Tropical Wellness Secrets

Tropical Wellness Secrets

Global Health
& Lifestyle Practices
& Recipes
Infused with Caribbean Style

by ANNICK LEWIS

My Green Balance

Barbados

EAT BEAUTIFUL AND THRIVE

Table of CONTENTS

PART I: IDEAS & INFORMATION

PART II: RECIPES

The Recipe for Success : Creating Healthy and Delicious Meals

BEVERAGES

PRODUCTIVE FUEL

GORGEOUS GREENS

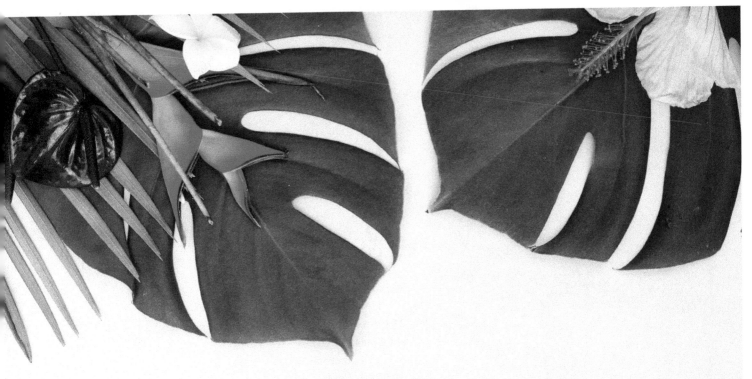

SEXY COCKTAILS

SWEET TOOTH SOLUTIONS

CONCLUSION: YOUR PATH TO WELLNESS

Acknowledgements

FOREWORD

I finally feel ready to share my curated list of wellness secrets that I have gathered over the past 12 years in wellness study and coaching. This book is the perfect addition to your home for wellness inspiration. Whether you are an elite athlete or a health beginner, there always comes a day where a little inspiration can lead to a lot of motivation.

Thank you for welcoming me as a keepsake into your home. Community and tribes are essential for health and wellness and we can keep healthier together. I feel your tribe will love when you share some of these wellness secrets from the tropics at your home while entertaining, or even at a social event. Treating yourself is always a good idea because we too often neglect self care so I will be here to share these moments of care with you, and when you do feel more social, your tribe will be pleased.

I have always been curious about Hollywood beauty and fitness secrets so I have paid close attention to the fashion and media industry. Seeing that these glamor looks came with a variety of experts and advice, I paid extra close attention to the likes of the diet, fitness, and beauty regimes of the Elite and World Class Athletes.

The Caribbean is a popular destination for world travelers and actors, athletes, and pop stars. Our diet is so multicultural with many flavors to be enjoyed for our human existence. Being raised in the tropics, I became curious to see how we could attain these beauty and fitness standards in a more sustainable manner and using natural and local ingredients mostly.

There are some great stories that I hope you enjoy that will take you on a journey with me but also captivate your mind with the top secrets of keeping lean and healthy. There are many ingredients that have been kept the top secret in town and I have included some of my personal favorite recipes as well as recipes created with friends and family. These recipes are meant to indulge your palette but keep your waistline in mind.

2

INTRODUCING...
A STORY ABOUT
ORGANNICK

ABOUT THE AUTHOR

As a child growing up in the Caribbean, I was very sick. I had a lot of allergies to different foods, and I struggled with emotional turbulence. That's why I'm so passionate about helping people improve their lives and finding health and balance within themselves and their environments and communities as individuals. When people have a healthy diet and lifestyle and feel grounded in themselves, they are more capable of solving real life problems. Wellness is a lifelong journey.

I believe the tropical setting and island culture of the Caribbean offers the world surprising secrets that can help anybody achieve a healthier body, mindset, and emotional/spiritual self, no matter where they live. In this book, we will explore the six principles or habits that come naturally to people who live in the tropics. These healthy habits promote a balance in both eating and lifestyle and can be implemented and applied anywhere in the world.

As the youngest of four offspring and the youngest girl—the daughter of a diplomat father with lots of social obligations and a Catholic mother who was very controlling—I grew up in a confining environment. My mother was very dogmatic, overseeing what we ate and what we did, and trying to nurture our spiritual gifts as well. My father's job required us to host a lot of parties, as well as attend a variety of events, which put us in the public eye a lot and demanded certain standards of behavior. We constantly had tasks, schedules, and people visiting. I needed time to relax and that was not an option.

INTRODUCING ANNICK LEWIS

A natural instinct in my personality is to be competitive and I wanted to win everything. I wouldn't settle for anything less than first place distinctions in gymnastics and ballet. In my friend group, I felt left out because of the demanding schedule that I kept and because my mother wouldn't let us eat junk food and sweets. I was made to feel like a showoff because this is how I knew to have fun, by practicing my tumbles in public spaces. I had gymnastics and ballet friends who were all high achievers, and they understood the dynamic of my life, but I had other friends who didn't take those activities seriously and I rejected them more than I would like to admit. I could be the mean girl sometimes.

Before the age of eleven, I was very allergic to milk and artificial colors. I had asthma and used ventilators. At that age, your friends are eating junk food and sweets. It was emotionally challenging because I wanted to eat like everybody else. I would binge on milk and dairy and sugar. I always thought, *Oh, I'm not sick anymore, I can drink it now, it's fine*, and then it would happen again. It was a continuous cycle of restriction and binging. Whenever I ate what normal people ate, I would get coughs, colds, and bronchitis.

My parents divorced when I was eleven. There was so much change in that two-year gap. My mom was distraught, and my older siblings changed their lives and became independent. My dad fell in love and moved far away. I felt abandoned. I quit gymnastics and ballet, and lost interest in sports. My mom was not supportive of my relationship with my father. When my dad decided he wanted me to sail, I did it to be close to him. We had a coach from Peru come in to stay with us. He was very strict and I had to be very disciplined in my eating habits, working out, and sailing three or four days a week in heavy winds. It was very intense and I cried a lot in the process but I was the number one female sailer in Trinidad.

My weight from 13 to 18 fluctuated. There was no real emotional support except from my friends and food. So my appetite increased. I would eat a bit too much, and sometimes the wrong things. I ate a lot of pastas and yoghurts and granolas, chocolates and milks and fried foods. I would stay at my friends' homes eating "normal" food, enjoying sweets or candies. I became quite rebellious. I started smoking marijuana when I was about sixteen to numb all of my emotions. I snuck out to parties with my friends quite often. I was moody and had a lot of tantrums and emotional breakdowns. And I started getting a lot of joint pain early on. I felt like I was an old person in a young person's body.

The turning point came when I moved to England. I had decided to go to Oxford Brookes University at seventeen because I graduated early. I'm not sure my brain was developed enough to process the change from a Caribbean lifestyle to life at Oxford without the parental support that was required to perform well. My mom did make the effort to settle me in to university but then she had to go back to the Caribbean and I didn't keep in much contact with her. In the meantime, my dad remarried, then he had my half-sister.

Financially I was struggling, and school was hard for me. My mother was not adept in emotional support and in language communication since her first language was French and my dad was never able to fix any problem I needed to solve. When he sent money, it always came with a lecture, or it was late, and that put me in some difficult situations. I wanted to be successful so badly but the first two years were really challenging. I turned to partying and smoking a lot of weed. Even when I started eating healthfully, I would still smoke a lot of weed.

I realized I wanted to be slim and I didn't want to be sick anymore. I stopped eating junk food and tried gluten- and dairy-free foods. A friend gave me a book on eating vegan, which I tried for a while, and that introduced me to the idea that women around the world were eating this way. Like most young girls, I would look at magazines and imagine looking like that. So I had my share of vanity, wanting to stay slim and look good. But ultimately the turning point was the level of sickness I was experiencing. I began practicing whole food recipes and letting my roommates test-taste them. They enjoyed my cooking, which make me feel confident about eating healthfully.

I earned a personal training certification before I left Oxford. When I moved back to Trinidad, I discovered there weren't many healthy options. I was at my leanest weight that year, and I was getting a lot of attention, working at a top Pilates studio. But at 21, my high school friends were so excited to have me back, they wanted to party. I wanted a career but I also wanted a social life. I couldn't seem to do both. Even though my mom was supportive, she was not able to communicate with me emotionally. At that time, my sister also moved back from England, so there were three women in the house. Everybody was overweight. I found that if I was to fix myself, I couldn't be in my mom's environment, so I moved out. At home, I wasn't allowed to get my hair done or wear lipstick. I wasn't allowed to spend money on clothing but I had to invest my money in my mom's house. I would have loved to have my father or a female mentor show me how to stand up for myself. Moving out of the house and in with two ladies who were Caribbean, I learned about style, fashion, beauty, makeup, etc. I was also able to save to travel to conferences since I didn't have to pay rent. That helped me evolve.

I started one of the first food delivery businesses in Trinidad, delivering gluten-free, dairy-free dishes made by a chef I knew from a cruise ship. The business was set up to be a success until my mother started planting seeds that I couldn't trust these people. They were trustworthy, but I went into a downward spiral. That kept happening to me. Just on the verge of success, I would end up bailing. Doing lots of therapy helped me feel like I could push through to complete whatever I was doing. But I do have tendencies to run away from my success when I'm in the middle of something. I'm working through growing more, thinking bigger, pushing through. I decided not to collaborate with teams or look for investors, but to fund everything myself, and be self-reliant.

I had to remove certain mindsets to understand who to trust and who not to trust so I can move forward, guided by my intuition. When I sacrificed my social life, I learned that your brain keeps developing until you are 25. I felt so dumb after I graduated that I decided to spend all my time studying. I read everything. I started consuming audio books, podcasts, business books, entrepreneurship books, leadership books, and of course, all the health and nutrition books. Ten years later, I am a product of that compounded knowledge. Eventually, I wanted to be with my boyfriend at the time so I moved to Barbados. His mom and sister were also into health and fitness. His sister was a trainer and she gave me a good perspective on natural nutrition and fitness from her studies in Canada. It felt like a good environment where I could grow and feel supported. When that relationship ended, I moved to the west coast and made a life of my own, making relationships with top chefs and wellness coaches who have inspired me along the way.

I started testing a lot of recipes, using different cooking methods, trying to figure out what tasted good. I started going to conferences and doing research into diets around the world. I studied what people were doing in Italy where people live the longest, or in California where health gurus were popular. But I looked around and thought, *In the Caribbean, we have all these great ingredients, naturally, and not many people are thinking about how to integrate or use them.* We have coconuts and can make coconut flour, or mangos and papayas, we eat a lot of greens, or avocado on toast, or rice cakes. We have black rice, plantains, breadfruit, sweet potatoes, all of which are some favorites. The greens that are consumed here are great but you need to consume bigger quantities than what you would typically do in a Caribbean meal. A recipe guide that I would give to my clients inspired the recipes included in this book. Clients wanted to be healthy but they didn't understand how to make healthy food taste good. Because of my experimentation, I understood how to make healthy food taste good using Caribbean ingredients.

During this time period, I also started developing my ideas around pillars of health and what secrets the Caribbean offers for health and wellness that any client, from anywhere, could adapt. These are the parts of us that we want to cultivate through our evolution as individuals. These areas encompass hydration, diet, fitness, sleep, spiritual growth, and emotional and psychological wellbeing.

In the following chapters, I'll explore these principles, offering recipes that revolve around these principles, derived from the healthiest of Caribbean lifestyles.

1. Island culture emphasizes community while allowing space for solitude.
2. Tropical living and island culture create an environment conducive to a healthy life/work balance.
3. Connecting to the elements regularly gives us the distance we need from stress. It also calms us down and helps us regulate ourselves emotionally and psychologically.
4. Island culture invites people to get outdoors and be active—a key component to being healthy in body and mind.
5. Eat with a tropical mindset: eat foods that are refreshing and take a whole foods approach for both beauty and longevity.
6. Due to the sun, heat, and humidity in tropical areas, people naturally gravitate towards hydrating their bodies. Water helps all our systems and internal organs operate in the best way possible.

ALLURE OF THE TROPICAL LIFESTYLE

Island culture emphasizes community while allowing
space for solitude.

Growing up in Trinidad, we would go to friends' homes during mango season to pick mangos and make mango chow, a semi-ripe mango seasoned with lime and fresh herbs and salt. It serves as a cool fresh fruit snack, popular in the Caribbean. That was a fun, friend-time snack. I remember driving around Queens Park Savannah with friends and picking up a fresh, cold coconut to drink. I love having a chat with friends while drinking coconut water, perhaps walking around the Savannah together. Now, even in solitude, food prevails. There's nothing like making a warm almond-milk latte or a fresh cup of tea at home, or getting kombucha and feeling happy in my own environment as I sip a drink. You should never really eat alone, but sometimes it's unavoidable. So prioritize your health....There is a balance between spending time with our communities and spending time alone. Principle number one for this book is the way that tropical or island culture emphasizes community while allowing space for solitude.

Community

Community is a fundamental human need. People have to feel like they're part of something to be fulfilled. You can join a sports club, go to church, take an art class, or join a leisure center or take up a hobby. You can volunteer as part of a charity or society or join a book club, or become involved in your neighborhood with friends and neighbors. It's healthy to be part of a group that allows you to grow as well as feel safe. Growth doesn't have to stop just because you reach a certain age. We are always growing if we choose to. Community can be the source of acceptance to allow you to evolve.

Food and conversation build trust and safety. Sitting around a meal creates the possibility to make that human connection we crave, to create a place of mutual support, compassion, and empathy, where you feel nourished both physically and emotionally. Conversation is what's important in these moments—catching up, finding out what the kids are up to, having mindful conversations.

Yet a healthy balance for communities includes activities. You can introduce interactive social events to a meal with family and friends. Kayaking or swimming on a beach day, playing games around the table, having quiz nights, walking dogs on the beach, hiking, boating or going ice-skating or snowshoeing if you live in cold regions. You can introduce these things into your current community, but sometimes, you might need to change environments if some people or places are not healthy influences on you, whether that's psychologically or emotionally or physically. Noticing which environments make us feel recharged is one of the secrets to wellness. Choose those activities and spaces consistently for fulfillment and happiness.

Solitude

All humans have an inner monk. Because society is so noisy, we don't always have the opportunity to tune in to what's really going on inside our hearts, souls, and minds, to understand ourselves on a deeper level.

Spending time in nature, going for a walk, visiting a botanical garden, or listening to ocean waves, are all ways that remind us what it means to be human. Solitude allows us time to reflect and experience our emotions, especially if we're moving through things like grief, or if life is stressful.

Healthy solitude includes laying out under the stars on a lounge chair, listening to music or podcasts. It can look like wrapping up in a cozy blanket and watching candlelight, watching a favorite movie or series, going for a walk, reading a book, practicing meditation or prayers. You can start knitting or cooking, or art, or gardening. Even cleaning can be a healthy way to practice solitude. But it's good to avoid unhealthy forms of solitude—doing a lot of drugs, being unproductive for too long, failing to uphold your responsibilities, not having a proper schedule, wasting time, watching too much tv, playing too many video games, eating too much junk food or too much food in general, not exercising.

A tropical life encourages a slower pace of life. It forces you to be patient, to go with the flow of nature. We all have a vision of lying on a hammock near the beach. That doesn't mean being lazy but enjoying the ocean breeze, enjoying the warmth. You need that slow time to rest. If you don't live in the tropics, then apply it to sitting in a lounge chair on the porch, laying outside, watching the sunset. Learn what soothes YOU, whether that's mediation or reading a book or going into your room for time out for a little while.

With solitude, you learn how you operate as an individual, which helps you when you want to operate as a couple or family. Even in a group setting, you still want to keep a level of individuality. No matter what, at the end of a busy day, give yourself half an hour to be in slowness, however that looks. Community and solitude have to co-exist as they are both important for our well-being. The secret to fulfilling intimate relationships is to get to know yourself and allow vulnerability in communicating to create deeper level connections.

EMBRACING TROPICAL LIVING : CREATING HEALTHY LIFE/WORK BALANCE

Tropical living and island culture create an environment conducive to a healthy life/work balance.

Somebody I met this weekend told me that I definitely come across like an island girl. I think he felt like my vibe was slow and relaxed, as opposed to a person who lives in a city who has a vibe that is go-go-go. Tropical living and island culture naturally create an environment conducive to a healthy life/work balance: the invitation of the ocean and the world "outside" means individuals are more likely to create a lifestyle with periods of work, periods of relaxation, and periods of rest—a more healthy way to live overall.

Slow living is a fundamental part of tropical life. Like the slow food movement in Italy, our culture tends to take its time with things, not to rush. We are present in the moment, especially when it comes to meals and socializing. It's hard for many people with distractions everywhere to slow down. That's why meditation is so important. That's why taking time to eat and spend time with your family is important. That's why spending time in nature is important. You need to disconnect (from the busy work world) to be able to be in the present moment.

A lot of communication break-downs are around the challenges of successful human-tech integration. If you're trying to build deep human connections, tech can get in the way of that human moment. The secret is that there are different learning styles and communication styles. Some personalities are more present with tech and some are more present without tech. Each human craves human connections where people can be present with them, so you must find out how you can create better connections with your friends, with or without tech. Learning how to tune in to the present moment helps with this self-awareness skill.

Because we've grown up in a society where attention spans are limited, or people lack time, to be present all the time in this day and age feels impossible. Everybody has insecurities. Some people drink to relax and be vulnerable, or use recreational drugs for confidence, which is all fleeting in the end. When you're not surrounded by a trusted community, to build deep connections initially without the aid of substances can make you feel anxious. Pulling out your phones to take a picture can be a healthy way to integrate technology into relationships and give you the opportunity to check out of being too present for a few moments. It's a fine balance. We're meant to be around each other, we're tribal, yet it can be draining to always be giving energy to someone. Sometimes zoning out of a conversation, to be on a phone, is a way to recharge your energy, but it can come across as rude. And you can get benefits of being in nature or being around someone without being in direct connection with them.

Some people think work-life balance is a myth. But we have to slow down sometimes, and then pick up the pace sometimes. If we consider the idea of masculine and feminine energies and cycles, this can help us understand the need to schedule a healthy, balanced lifestyle. The female cycle is a natural way for women to balance their social lives and their need for solitude. Men don't have the hormonal changes women have, but their testosterone peaks during the day. Men typically can go-go-go more but that doesn't mean their social batteries will be charged all the time. Their work-life balance has to include making time for fitness and health and yoga so they can be healthy for their families. You can't have it all, or you can't have it all at once—something has to give. You don't want to give up your health, and you don't want to give up the money either, so where is time for family, friends, and community? The secret is work-life integration more so than work-life balance.I believe very much in quantifying your schedule. Scheduling all the priorities into your calendar is the way to make sure something gets done, but it also allows you to be flexible. You can break that structure, you're not bound to the structure, but discipline is freedom. I learned this from my favorite author Brendon Burchard and it has changed my life and helps with my clients' lives.

Once an activity—whether it's work, or fitness, or time with friends, or even just walking your dog—is in the calendar and part of your structured day, you can allow life to flow more freely. Know yourself as a person and track your time. Understand when you need to socialize, when you need to rest, when you need to work out. Some psychology suggests that people get sick because they have been pushing themselves too hard; their body subconsciously forces them to rest. Your schedule should allow for rest and rejuvenation—whether it occurs on a weekly schedule or a monthly schedule. The more we are mentally doing things and focused and engaged in the moment with things that fill our cup as humans—whether that's connecting to your spirit, reading, art, writing, music, exercise, communicating with people, reaching out—these things can be aligned with our purpose. And also it filters out low-quality experiences. It's good to have the mindset of being in monk mode. It's OK to be silent sometimes, and to be alone. You don't always have to talk.

An unhealthy part of island culture is the lack of boundaries. There is no acknowledgment that you are not in service to everyone around you all the time. You are a member of the community, yes, but the relationship with the self has to come first for health and wellness. This secret—taking care of the self—allows you to show up in society, personal relationships, and communities to make a difference and to feel good about yourself. This is an important component of functional living. The more humans can master themselves, the more impact they can make in the world. Once you're healthy and well, you can provide better quality service to others.

Finally, it's important to realize that the environment and space around us affects how we live. In my personal experience, living with my mom was uncomfortable and unhealthy. Now I live in a very peaceful environment—a cottage with an ocean view. It's very quiet and allows me to have that monk experience. Don't be afraid to change where and how you live, if you are unhappy or find it isn't contributing to your health and wellness.

RESTORATIVE POWER OF THE TROPICS: CONNECTING TO THE ELEMENTS AND NATURE

Connecting to the elements regularly gives us the distance we need from stress. It also calms us down and helps us regulate ourselves emotionally and psychologically.

When we're stressed, our minds repeat stories or worries. We get sucked into a continuous reel and it stresses our whole body out. We have to learn how to separate our experience from our thoughts. Instead of numbing out, you can learn to create a safe space to detach naturally. Connecting to nature or the elements (earth, water, air, fire, and the ethers or space) regularly, preferably daily, gives us the distance we need from stress. It also calms us down and helps us regulate ourselves emotionally and psychologically.

You can connect to the elements anywhere in the world, no matter where you live.

Tap into the five senses. Use essential oils or light candles with natural scents like fresh mint. You can put nature sounds on your phone or stereo system and listen to ocean waves crashing or palm trees swaying with birds chirping. You can go to a massage or a spa. You can also cocoon yourself in cozy materials, whether it's wrapping yourself in a warm blanket or wearing cottons to keep you cool or snug and warm. Experiencing the ocean breeze, and feeling the wind in your hair, is one of the most relaxing parts of being in the tropics. It can make you feel carefree and take you out of the stressful parts of your day-to-day life. Enjoying the heat of a coastal bonfire with friends, while listening to the sounds of the waves and roasting breadfruits in the fire, looking at flames combusting, can be part of letting go and processing change. When it comes to bodies of water, there are pools, oceans, and rivers, streams and waterfalls. Each of these bodies of water give a different understanding or experience of being human and to feeling cleansed and recharged. Even a bath in the comfort of your home can bring that sense of renewal. For the ethers, having spatial awareness of your human body in the environment around you. Looking at the stars and planets in the night sky can give a sense of the relationship between human and space, whether that's the space in front of us or the space of the universe. Walking barefoot is the best way to connect to the earth, to feel grounded when life is changing. You can walk on the beach, plant a garden, visit an orchard and pick a fruit, hang out with a pet or family outside. These are all things that bring human comfort when we're experiencing the hardships of day-to-day life or traveling too much.

Spend time in nature. Connecting to nature is about connecting to ourselves. No matter where you live, you can find ways to spend time in nature or access the elements. Go for walks with the dog, go skiing, take a hike in the mountains, or sit by the ocean or a lake. If it's cold outside, light a fire pit or candles and watch the snow falling. If you live in a very urban or harsh environment, you can still create a space to connect with nature, even if that means bringing nature and plants into your home. Go to sleep with audio sounds of rivers flowing, or birds chirping, or waves crashing on a beach. If you live in the desert, you can create a stone garden or labyrinth. If you don't have a view that is natural, then create something in your space that relaxes you. Laying out under the moon or stars is one of my favorite go-tos after a stressful day or night. It is easy to forget that nature is sometimes at our doorstep for a quick recharging escape. Shooting stars are one of those experiences that can feel magical and exciting and bring delight into our lives.

Meditation and breath work. Being in the present moment can help us slow down and manage our stressful thoughts so that we don't turn to overeating or over-indulging in drugs, sex, gambling, or risky behaviors as ways to cope. When we're consumed with worry or stress, or a negative story is running through our minds, breath work and meditation help us to focus and be in the present moment. They calm the nervous system and put distance between reality and our psychological experience of it.

Focus on imagining your own mental challenges as a garden space. Pull out the weeds of thought that are bothering you or recurring patterns of stress, and sprinkle seeds of new thoughts, calming reminders, new patterns. Breath work is the watering of that process. It breathes life into the body, it's cleansing, it gives us clarity and allows us to show up in the present moment and let go of the heavy thoughts that weigh us down.

Create an environment and space that contributes to your well-being and health. Your daily environment needs to be set up so that it contributes to your daily needs of both energy and rest. The place we live in needs to be a functional space. If it's not, it makes it harder to become and stay healthy. Work to create spaces at home for relaxation and healthy habits, whether that's a porch for chilling out after a long day or a cozy movie room or creating a garden. You might need a sanctuary room where you have your prayer things and candles, a meditation pillow, a yoga mat, rosaries, prayer beads, books, a reading room. Feeling safe in an environment is a prime component of being healthy and creating a sense of being safe in the body. The secret is having a sense of groundedness, boundaries, privacy, and comfort in the home. Energy is a priority and our environment plays a huge role in a peaceful energy flow.

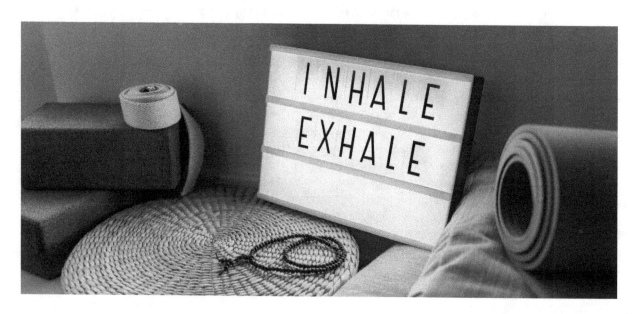

MINDFULNESS AND MOVEMENT IN THE TROPICS: GETTING OUTDOORS, BEING ACTIVE

Tropical culture invites people to get outdoors and be active—a key component to being healthy in body and mind.

We need to connect to our bodies. Exercise and movement takes us out of our minds and puts us in tune with our bodies, puts us in the present moment, and releases stress. One of the benefits of the tropical world and island culture is that it invites people to be active, outdoors. Combining activity with connecting to nature motivates people to stay fit. If you have struggled with fitness, particularly if you live in a very cold or very hot region, or perhaps the outside world around you is not particularly beautiful, you need to find reasons and ways to get up and get moving.

People who are just beginning may feel intimidated by the idea of going to the gym. If that's you, start simply with walking outside or going for a swim. Anything that makes you active is a win. For motivation, you have to visualize activity as part of your lifestyle. That's why the gym routine can feel intimidating, but when you think about it as part of your routine, part of your everyday life, and you've committed time in your schedule for activity 3-4 days a week, then it's something you get done, similar to how you take a shower every day, or clean your house. There has to be a mental shift: this is something you do every day. Motivation comes and goes but habits and routines are what make us what we are.

You may also need an identity shift. Begin to think of yourself as more athletic, not as fat or sick. You don't have to think "I'm a runner" if you're not a runner. Maybe you're a dancer, maybe you're a swimmer. Choose something for your personality that you can stick with.

And try different types of exercise—tennis, pickleball, sailing. The point is to pick something that suits YOUR lifestyle. Then you can be consistent. Schedule it but be flexible.

As I've mentioned in previous chapters, connect to green spaces as much as possible. Ride your bike outside. In many places, you can go hiking in the mountains, or walk to waterfalls. You can go swimming, go for walks, play golf, or jog. Keeping active with sports is obviously a good idea. The concept of "grounding" comes into play here. You want to connect your feet to the earth by walking on the beach, putting your toes in the water, walking on grass, or gardening. These activities burn calories but also help keep us grounded. If you can't go anywhere, you can do yoga or Pilates at home, or have exercise equipment at home. Dancing is always great. You can listen to the sounds of nature on your phone while you're at the gym or on the treadmill. In order to keep something up long term, you have to do it at different intensities. Some days, you may have more energy and you can put in hard effort at the gym, but another day you may take it easy and go for a walk. It depends on what your body is calling for each day. Even on restful days, keep moving, stretching, etc. Think of activity as a dial on the radio. It's always on but you can move the volume up or down. Life is always changing. The goal is to do something active no matter where you are, most days of the week.

I like to mix it up. I get bored of doing the same thing. Sometimes when I travel, I'll find a class, or when I'm home, I'll go for a walk one day and a jog another day and a swim another day. But I also like going to the gym sometimes, if friends are going. If you have people who want to hang out with you but you want to stay healthy, you can go walking or play tennis together instead of hanging out at the bar. It helps you to keep a social connection while moving.

Some people look to travel with healthy options and healthy activities wherever they're staying. Some people want to travel and sit on a beach and eat and drink. But if you are to tap into the island culture, or if you're traveling to anywhere in the tropics, you want to prioritize walking, or swimming, or some kind of activity to recharge your body and give yourself a real vacation. The beautiful secrets await you in the sounds of the trees rustling, the night sky, the birds chirping, the crickets at night, reminding you that you are never alone and a mindful oasis is there for you on demand. Then you can go back to your corporate or city life, knowing that you are recharged and can implement a routine of walking regularly. The secret is that in more relaxed environments, we feel a little more confident to try new routines, whether that's on the weekend or while traveling. Sometimes we have to create a habit on vacation before we can bring it back to our lives.

POWER OF WHOLE FOODS: NOURISHING WITH A TROPICAL MINDSET

Eat with a tropical mindset: eat foods that are refreshing, and take a whole foods approach for both beauty and longevity.

This weekend, I was invited out to go sailing. I packed a snack for the boat—baby carrots and hummus. When we went out after, it was amazing to find cassava and sweet potato crisps as well as breadfruit with guacamole on top. This whole foods way of eating helps you stay youthful and healthy.

The Caribbean is known for its flavor. These days, you can find tropical ingredients in grocery stores around the world, and many of the most exciting, healthful, refreshing foods are from the tropics. Breadfruit and cassava are root vegetables that serve as superfoods. There are so many fruits and vegetables: avocado, mango, coconut, pineapple, herbs, lettuces, papaya, cucumber. Coconut water is obviously fantastic. These are prime ingredients for health and longevity. We also have access to really healthy seafood—fish in the oceans are really clean. Greens like callaloo and bok choy are easy to integrate into a diet. If you need gluten-free alternatives, you can find flour made from cassava or breadfruit. These foods are very functional and medicinal. They are good for digestion and our immune system; they give us energy and mental clarity, and they contribute to longevity.

These foods may only be at specialty stores or you may feel they are not part of your budget, but you are investing in your health and this will prevent medical bills in the future. Plus these foods help bring out your natural beauty. You can find other ingredients in different marketplaces, like Indian markets. There, you can find lentils and beans and peas, which help reduce cardiovascular disease. Seafood has a lot of omega 3s. If you're in a place where you go spearfishing with friends, you are keeping active while making healthy, sustainable choices. When you travel to the Caribbean, eat seafood instead of going for the typical Alfredo pasta.

People often think of rice and peas, macaroni pie, and dumplings when they think of Caribbean food but just like Hawaii, we have an abundance of natural, whole foods to choose from. I like to grill zucchini and squash, that's literally my favorite way to bbq. You can make fresh salsas, ceviches with fresh herbs, lemons, limes. The tropical world has different salsas. It's easy to make poke bowls at home or create taco shells from breadfruit to replace the corn. The secret here is to use lots of herbs and spices to get the best flavors to make your nutritional food as delicious as possible without adding calories and fat.

Tropical meals should feel refreshing. Grilled, lean, with a lot of fresh ingredients, citrusy salads, and vibrant herbs. Keep it simple and fresh. A fun tip: spice up your life with the Caribbean flavors.

THE FLOW OF WATER: REJUVENATION OF THE MIND, BODY, AND SOUL

Due to the sun, heat, and humidity in tropical areas, people naturally gravitate towards hydrating their bodies. Water helps all our systems and internal organs operate in the best way possible.

The body is about 70% water, so we need water consistently to make sure all of our systems and organs operate the best way they can. Water gives us more energy and reduces our cravings for food and sweets. It helps us control our portion sizes. For people who are overweight or looking to lose weight, the first priority is building a water habit because overeating usually comes from a place of dehydration. If we feel irritable or anxious, sometimes water is a good solution to calm our bodies down. It's an overlooked resource to consider for keeping yourself grounded and calm. And some people think it's fun to have water as an emotional support tool. If you carry your reusable water bottle wherever you go, you will feel comfortable in different environments. Make drinking water fun and prioritize it.

Hydration can come in a lot of forms: water, watery vegetables like cucumbers, coconut water, teas. You can drink sparkling water or put berries in your water. You can create a variety of spa waters, like cutting up cucumbers or lemons to add to your H2O fun habit. Instead of going for snacks and chocolates and different indulgences, have water as a choice when you fill up your fridge, or as one of the choices you make if you're on a road trip or out for a drive.

Given your daily schedule, find a hydration habit that works for you. Begin the day flushing out the body with water, so you're starting your body with an essential nutrient. As soon as you wake up in the morning, drink water. You can set that up on your nightstand before you go to bed. Similarly you can drink water before bed unless it causes you to wake up to go to the bathroom. In general, have a routine.

Quality does matter. Filtered water is always going to be the most favorable choice. Some water filters have filtration processes that get rid of dirt and chemicals, and some actually promote more minerals in the water as well. If you can't filter your water, then buy bottled water, but be mindful of the environment and recycle used bottles.

The recommended amount is half the body weight in ounces.

The islands offer experiences to be in the oceans. You can swim some laps, bathe under a waterfall, sit in island homes overlooking the seas, dip in lagoons, kayak or fish in rivers, or take scenic drives by the water. These are all ways in which to enjoy the vibe of water and relaxation. For full rejuvenation, it is best to immerse yourself by swimming, diving, and even just floating in the water. This experience reminds us that to alleviate stress, we want to embody the flow of water, even for a few minutes of the day. The secret here is to observe and experience water. Water comes and goes, tides ebb and flow. Understanding water helps us to understand the way to navigate the changes of life, through both times of calm and smooth sailing or during times of high waters and storms. Even in unpredictable situations, you can find the stillness within by understanding how water flows and moves. This is why people say that if you're worried, you should go to the beach. Water allows us to let go of our thoughts and naturally brings us into the present moment.

SLOW MORNING

BEVERAGES

WAKE ME UP WITH A KISS

ORGANNICK'S HOT CHOCOLATE

Ingredients

1 cup almond milk.
1-2 tbsp, honey or sweetener
or choice.
1 dash cinnamon.
2 tbsp cocoa powder.
1 dash himalayan salt.

Directions

1 Heat the almond milk in a small saucepan over medium heat until hot, but not boiling.

2 Add in the brown sugar or sweetener of choice and whisk until fully dissolved.

3 Whisk in the cocoa powder and cinnamon until fully combined.

4 Add a dash of Himalayan salt and continue whisking until the mixture is smooth and creamy.

5 Pour the hot cocoa into a mug and enjoy!

Optional: Top with whipped cream or marshmallows for an extra indulgent treat.

This drink is great for a morning but you can also enjoy a cozy self-care hot choc, solo evening catching up on your favorite reads or movies.

Alternatively, this recipe is a fave for sleepovers & warm friendly catch ups.

Here are the approximate nutrition facts for one serving (using almond milk and 1 tablespoon of brown sugar):

Calories: 95
Total Fat: 5g
Saturated Fat: 1g
Trans Fat: 0g
Cholesterol: 0mg
Sodium: 100mg
Total Carbohydrates: 15g
Dietary Fiber: 3g
Sugars: 10g
Protein: 3g

Please note that these values may vary depending on the specific brand of ingredients used and the amount of sweetener added.

ALMOND LATTE

Ingredients

1/2 Cup Almond Milk
3/4 Cup Brewed Coffee
1 Tbsp Sweetener of choice

Directions

1   Brew 3/4 cup of coffee using your preferred brewing method.

2   While the coffee is brewing, heat 1/2 cup of almond milk in a small saucepan over a medium heat. Heat until the milk is warm but not boiling.

3   Once the coffee is brewed, pour it into a large mug.

4   Add 1 tablespoon of honey to the brewed coffee and stir until the honey is fully dissolved.

5   Pour the warm almond milk into the mug with the coffee.

6   Use a whisk or a handheld frother to froth the milk until it is creamy and frothy.

7   Sprinkle some ground cinnamon or cocoa powder on top for extra flavor.

8   Serve and enjoy your delicious Almond Milk Honey Coffee!

Here are the approximate nutrition facts for one serving of Almond Milk Honey Coffee:

Calories: 71
Total Fat: 2g
Saturated Fat: 0g
Trans Fat: 0g
Cholesterol: 0mg
Sodium: 65mg
Total Carbohydrates: 12g
Dietary Fiber: 1g
Sugars: 10g
Protein: 1g

Please note that these values may vary depending on the specific brand of ingredients used and the amount of honey added.

Optional: You can add a pinch of ground cinnamon or nutmeg to the coffee before adding the almond milk for extra flavor.

Enjoy this one as you start your day, sit and chill in your garden or look out at your view sipping the indulgent yumminess of dairy free life while you energize your morning. I add some stevia usually or monk fruit as my sweetener but you may like honey.

ICED COFFEE FOR BITCHY POOS

Ingredients

1 cup almond milk.
1/2 cup Coffee Pressed.
1 Tbsp Honey (optional)
1 cup of Ice.

Directions

1 Brew 1/2 cup of coffee using your preferred method. Alternatively, you can use cold brewed coffee if you have it on hand.

2 Add 1 cup of ice to a tall glass.

3 Pour 1 cup of unsweetened almond milk over the ice.

4 Add the brewed coffee to the glass and stir well.

5 If desired, add 1 tbsp of honey and stir until dissolved.

6 Serve immediately and enjoy your delicious iced coffee with almond milk!

This is my favorite go-to when meeting up with a friend or client.

Alternatively, if it is an action-packed week then this is also a great go-to for getting into Boss Mode.

Here are the approximate nutrition facts for one serving of iced coffee with almond milk, assuming the use of 1 cup of unsweetened almond milk, 1/2 cup of coffee, 1 tbsp of honey (optional), and 1 cup of ice:

Calories: 35
Total Fat: 2 g
Saturated Fat: 0 g
Trans Fat: 0 g
Cholesterol: 0 mg
Sodium: 90 mg
Total Carbohydrates: 5 g
Dietary Fiber: 1 g
Sugars: 3 g
Protein: 1 g

Note that the nutrition facts may vary slightly depending on the specific brands and types of ingredients used. The use of flavored syrups or other additions can also increase the calorie and sugar content of the drink. However, overall, this iced coffee with almond milk is a low-calorie and dairy-free alternative to traditional iced coffee drinks.

GOLDEN MILK

The Anti-Inflammatory Cozy Beverage

Ingredients

1 Cup Milk of Choice
1/2 Tsp Turmeric
1 Cinnamon Stick
1 Pinch Nutmeg
2 Tbsp Honey
1 Pinch Black Pepper

Directions

1   In a small saucepan, heat 1 cup of milk over low-medium heat until warm.

2   Add 1/2 tsp of ground turmeric to the milk and stir well.

3   Add 1 cinnamon stick to the milk and let it simmer for 5-10 minutes, stirring occasionally.

4   Add a pinch of ground nutmeg to the milk and stir well.

5   Remove the cinnamon stick from the milk and discard it.

6   Add 2 tbsp of honey to the milk and stir well.

7   Add a pinch of ground black pepper to the milk and stir well.

8   Pour the Golden Milk Latte into your favorite mug and serve hot.

9   Optionally, you can garnish with a sprinkle of cinnamon or nutmeg, if desired.

Enjoy your healthy and comforting Golden Milk Latte!

This recipe is a great way to incorporate the anti-inflammatory and antioxidant benefits of turmeric into your diet, and the addition of cinnamon and nutmeg gives it a delicious and warming flavor.

Calories: 120
Total Fat: 2.5 g
Saturated Fat: 0 g
Trans Fat: 0 g
Cholesterol: 0 mg
Sodium: 160 mg
Total Carbohydrates: 25 g
Dietary Fiber: 1 g
Sugars: 23 g
Protein: 1 g

Note that the nutrition facts may vary slightly depending on the specific brands and types of ingredients used. The type of milk used will also affect the calorie and nutrient content of the drink. However, overall, this Golden Milk Latte is a healthy and low-calorie alternative to traditional coffee or tea drinks, and it contains the anti-inflammatory and antioxidant benefits of turmeric.

LONDON FOG

Your favorite childhood drink — with a twist!

Ingredients

1 Earl Grey Tea bag
1/2 cup water
1/2 cup almond milk
1-2 tsp honey or sugar
(optional)
1/4 tsp vanilla extract
(optional)

Directions

1 Bring 1/2 cup of water to a boil in a small saucepan or kettle.

2 Once the water is boiling, remove it from the heat and add the Earl Grey Tea bag to the water.

3 Let the tea steep for 3-5 minutes or until desired strength is reached.

4 Remove the tea bag from the water and set aside.

5 In a separate saucepan, heat 1/2 cup of almond milk over low-medium heat, stirring occasionally to prevent scorching.

6 Once the almond milk is hot, whisk it until frothy using a milk frother, immersion blender, or whisk.

7 Pour the frothed almond milk into the tea and stir well.

8 Garnish with a sprinkle of cinnamon, if desired.

9 Serve hot and enjoy!

*This recipe makes one serving of London Fog with almond milk.
Feel free to adjust the sweetness or strength of the tea to your liking.
Enjoy your delicious and comforting London Fog!*

Calories: 45
Total Fat: 3 g
Saturated Fat: 0 g
Trans Fat: 0 g
Cholesterol: 0 mg
Sodium: 60 mg
Total Carbohydrates: 3 g
Dietary Fiber: 0 g
Sugars: 2 g
Protein: 1 g

Note that the nutrition facts may vary slightly depending on the specific brands and types of ingredients used.
The addition of honey or sugar will also increase the calorie and sugar content of the drink. However, overall, this London Fog recipe is a low-calorie and low-sugar alternative to traditional coffee or tea drinks, making it a great option for those who want a warm and comforting drink without the excess calories.

BEAUTY TEA

This Tea is Great to Energize Your Mind But Also For Skin Health.

Ingredients

Ingredients:
1 Hibiscus Tea bag
1 Green Tea bag
1/2 Lemon, sliced
4 cups of water

Directions

1 Bring 4 cups of water to a boil in a pot on the stove.

2 Add the Hibiscus Tea bag and Green Tea bag to the pot of boiling water.

3 Let the tea bags steep in the hot water for 5-7 minutes, or until desired strength is reached.

4 Remove the tea bags from the pot and discard them.

5 Squeeze the juice of half a lemon into the pot of tea and stir well.

6 Add the lemon slices to the tea and let steep for an additional 1-2 minutes.

7 Remove the lemon slices from the pot and discard them.

8 Pour the tea into your favorite teapot or cups, and serve hot.

9 You can also add some honey or sugar to taste, if desired.

Enjoy your delicious and refreshing Hibiscus Green Tea with Lemon!

Here are the approximate nutrition facts for a serving of Hibiscus Green Tea with Lemon, assuming a serving size of 1 cup (240 ml):
Calories: 5
Total Fat: 0 g
Saturated Fat: 0 g
Trans Fat: 0 g
Cholesterol: 0 mg
Sodium: 0 mg
Total Carbohydrates: 1 g
Dietary Fiber: 0 g
Sugars: 0 g
Protein: 0 g
Note that these nutrition facts may vary slightly depending on the specific brands of tea used and whether or not you add honey or sugar to the tea. However, overall, this tea is very low in calories and contains no fat, cholesterol, or sodium. It also contains some antioxidants and vitamins from the hibiscus, green tea, and lemon, making it a healthy and refreshing beverage option.

LEMON BERRY ICE TEA

Makes 4 servings

Ingredients

2 Berry Green Tea
2 Plain Green Tea
1 Lemon sliced in circles
1 cup boiling water
3 cups cold filtered water

Directions

1 Boil 1 cup of water in a kettle or on the stove.

2 Add 2 Berry Green Tea bags and 2 Plain Green Tea bags to a heat-safe pitcher.

3 Pour the boiling water over the tea bags and let steep for 3-5 minutes, or until desired strength is reached.

4 Remove the tea bags and discard.

5 Add 3 cups of cold filtered water to the pitcher and stir well.

6 Add the sliced lemon to the pitcher and stir gently.

7 Chill in the refrigerator for at least 1 hour, or until the tea is cold.

8 Serve over ice and enjoy your delicious and refreshing Berry Green Tea with lemon!

Here are the approximate nutrition facts for one serving of this Berry Green Tea with Lemon recipe, assuming the use of the specified ingredients and 8 servings in total:

Calories: 5
Total Fat: 0 g
Saturated Fat: 0 g
Trans Fat: 0 g
Cholesterol: 0 mg
Sodium: 1 mg
Total Carbohydrates: 1 g
Dietary Fiber: 0 g
Sugars: 0 g
Protein: 0 g

Note that the nutrition facts may vary slightly depending on the specific brands and types of ingredients used. Additionally, if you add any sweetener to the tea, such as honey, it will increase the calorie and sugar content of the drink. However, overall, this Berry Green Tea with Lemon is a low-calorie and healthy beverage that provides the antioxidant benefits of green tea and the refreshing taste of berries and lemon..

Note that you can adjust the amount of lemon to your liking, and you can also experiment with other types of fruit or herbs for added flavor. Additionally, you can sweeten the tea with honey or another sweetener if desired.

Enjoy your refreshing and healthy iced tea made with green tea, berries, and lemon!

LEMON BEAUTY

Enjoy this on a hot day while tending to your plant babies or chilling in the garden with one of your favourite books.

Ingredients

1 Rooibos Tea
1 Green or Black Caffeine Tea
1 Ginger Lemon Tea Bag
1 Lemon sliced
3 Slices Cucumber
1 Sprig Rosemary
1 Cups of Boiling water
3 cups cold filtered water
1-2 tbsp sweetener of choice

Here are the approximate nutrition facts for one serving of this Rooibos-Green Tea with Ginger, Lemon, Cucumber, and Rosemary recipe, assuming the use of the specified ingredients and 6 servings in total:Calories: 10
Total Fat: 0 g
Saturated Fat: 0 g
Trans Fat: 0 g
Cholesterol: 0 mg
Sodium: 2 mg
Total Carbohydrates: 3 g
Dietary Fiber: 1 g
Sugars: 1 g
Protein: 0 g
Note that the nutrition facts may vary slightly depending on the specific brands and types of ingredients used, as well as the amount of sweetener added. Additionally, this iced tea is a low-calorie and healthy beverage that provides the antioxidant benefits of rooibos and green tea, as well as the refreshing taste and nutrients of lemon, cucumber, and rosemary. Enjoy!

Directions

1 Boil 1 cup of water in a kettle or on the stove.

2 Add the Rooibos tea bag, Green or black tea bag, and Ginger lemon tea bag to a heat-safe pitcher.

3 Pour the boiling water over the tea bags and let steep for 3-5 minutes, or until desired strength is reached.

4 Remove the tea bags and discard.

5 Add 3 cups of cold filtered water to the pitcher and stir well.

6 Add the lemon slices, cucumber slices, and rosemary sprig to the pitcher and stir gently.

7 Chill in the refrigerator for at least 1 hour, or until the tea is cold.

8 Taste the tea and add sweetener of choice, if desired.

9 Serve over ice and enjoy your delicious and refreshing Rooibos-Green Tea with Ginger, Lemon, Cucumber, and Rosemary!

Note that you can adjust the amount of sweetener to your liking, and you can also experiment with other types of fruit or herbs for added flavor.

Additionally, you can use green or black tea depending on your preference or caffeine tolerance.

Enjoy your flavorful and healthy iced tea made with rooibos, green or black tea, ginger, lemon, cucumber, and rosemary!

ICED TEA

Iced Tea is one idea for summer drink. You can make it easily with recipe below and sip it to keep cool while enjoying some garden time.

Ingredients

1 ginger lemon tea bag
3 green tea bags
1 lemon
3 slices cucumber
1 sprig rosemary
4 cups of water
1-2 tsp sweetener of choice
your favorite glass.

Here are the estimated nutrition facts for one serving of the Ginger Lemon Green Tea with Cucumber and Rosemary recipe, without any added sweetener:
Calories: 5
Total Fat: 0g
Saturated Fat: 0g
Trans Fat: 0g
Cholesterol: 0mg
Sodium: 6mg
Total Carbohydrates: 1g
Dietary Fiber: 0g
Sugars: 0g
Protein: 0g
Note: The nutrition facts may vary slightly depending on the type and amount of sweetener you add to the tea. If you use a sweetener with calories, the calorie and sugar content will be higher.

Directions

1 In a large teapot or saucepan, bring 4 cups of water to a boil.

2 Once the water has boiled, turn off the heat and add the ginger lemon tea bag, green tea bags, and sliced lemon to the pot.

3 Let the tea steep for 3-5 minutes, depending on how strong you like your tea.

4 While the tea is steeping, add the cucumber slices and rosemary sprig to your favorite glass.

5 After the tea has steeped, remove the tea bags and lemon slices from the pot.

6 Stir in the sweetener of your choice until it has dissolved.

7 Pour the tea into the glass with the cucumber and rosemary.

8 Let the tea cool for a few minutes before enjoying!

Note: You can adjust the amount of sweetener to your liking, and you can also add more or less cucumber and rosemary depending on your preference. This recipe makes about 4 servings.

BREAKFAST TEA

Your favorite childhood
drink — with a twist!

Ingredients

1 Tea Bag
1 Tbsp Honey
Almond Milk to Taste

Directions

1 Boil water and steep 1 tea bag of your choice in a mug for 2-3 minutes, or until desired strength is reached.

2 Remove the tea bag and stir in 1 tbsp of honey until it's completely dissolved.

3 Add almond milk to taste and stir well.

4 Serve hot and enjoy your delicious Honey Almond Milk Tea!

Here are the approximate nutrition facts for one serving of Honey Almond Milk Tea, assuming the use of 1 tea bag, 1 tbsp of honey, and a splash of unsweetened almond milk:
Calories: 20
Total Fat: 0.5 g
Saturated Fat: 0 g
Trans Fat: 0 g
Cholesterol: 0 mg
Sodium: 5 mg
Total Carbohydrates: 4 g
Dietary Fiber: 0 g
Sugars: 4 g
Protein: 0 g
Note that the nutrition facts may vary slightly depending on the specific brands and types of ingredients used. The type and amount of almond milk used will also affect the calorie and nutrient content of the drink. However, overall, this Honey Almond Milk Tea is a low-calorie and healthy alternative to traditional tea drinks, and it provides the antioxidant benefits of tea and the nutrients of almond milk.

Note that you can adjust the amount of honey and almond milk to your liking.
You can also experiment with adding spices such as cinnamon, nutmeg, or ginger for extra flavor.

Enjoy your comforting and delicious Honey Almond Milk Tea, which is a great way to incorporate the health benefits of tea and almond milk into your diet!

MATCHA LATTE

Matcha Green Tea Lattes Hot & Cold

Ingredients

1 tsp Matcha powder
1 cup Dairy-free milk
1-2 tsp Hot water
Sweetener of choice
Optional 2 tbsp. Collagen powder

Directions

1 In a small bowl or cup, whisk together the matcha powder and hot water until there are no lumps.

2 In a small saucepan, heat the dairy-free milk over medium heat until hot, but not boiling.

3 Pour the hot milk into a blender, and add the matcha mixture and sweetener of your choice.

4 If using collagen powder, add it to the blender as well.

5 Blend the mixture until it's frothy and well-combined.

6 Pour the matcha latte into a mug and enjoy!

Here are the estimated nutrition facts for one serving of the Matcha Latte recipe with Collagen, using unsweetened almond milk as the dairy-free milk:
Calories: 98
Total Fat: 4.8g
Saturated Fat: 0.4g
Trans Fat: 0g
Cholesterol: 0mg
Sodium: 153mg
Total Carbohydrates: 8.5g
Dietary Fiber: 1.9g
Sugars: 5.6g
Protein: 6g
Note: The nutrition facts may vary depending on the type and brand of dairy-free milk and sweetener used. If you're using a sweetened dairy-free milk or a sweetener with calories, the calorie and sugar content will be higher. The addition of collagen powder increases the protein content.

Note: If you don't have a blender, you can use a whisk or a milk frother to combine the ingredients. You can also adjust the amount of hot water or milk to your liking, depending on how strong you like your matcha latte.

ENERGY SNACKS

PRODUCTIVE
FUEL YOUR MIND AND BODY
FUEL

GREEN SMOOTHIE

GREEN SMOOTHIE REVITALIZING

There's nothing like the feeling of a fresh green smoothie to start the day, especially when it is hot and you want to boost your energy. This is great to enjoy pre or post-workout and even on your way to work on a rushed day.

SERVINGS	TIME	DIFFICULTY	CALORIES
2	5 min	Easy	253 kcal

INGREDIENTS

½ cup of dairy free milk

½ cup coconut water

1/4 tsp matcha powder

1 frozen banana

1 handful spinach

2 pitted dates

1 tbsp honey

DIRECTIONS

1. Add the dairy-free milk and coconut water to a blender.
2. Add the matcha powder, frozen banana, spinach, dates, and honey to the blender.
3. Blend the ingredients on high speed until smooth and creamy.
4. Taste the smoothie and adjust the sweetness by adding more honey if desired.
5. Pour the smoothie into a glass and serve immediately.

NOTES

Green Smoothies are so revitalizing. Sometimes I swap out the frozen banana for pineapple or papaya, which are also very delicious. I would use 1/2 cup of frozen fruit for the best quality. Some people sub out the coconut water and or added sweeteners completely and that is totally up to you with how your taste buds enjoy. Mix it up so you never get bored.
Calories: 253 (with protein powder 391). Total Fat: 2.9g.
Saturated Fat: 0.7g. Trans Fat: 0g. Cholesterol: 0mg. Sodium: 115mg. Total Carbohydrates: 57.8g. Dietary Fiber: 6.1g.
Sugars: 39.2g. Protein: 4.2g (With 2 scoop Vegan Protein powder 18.3 g protein)

PAPAYA SMOOTHIE

PAPAYA MAMA   FRUITY BEAUTY

This is a beauty combintion for the books. Papaya is an ingredient that is in the top skin care brands and in reipes for that beautiful tropical glow.

SERVINGS
1-2

TIME
5-10 min

DIFFICULTY
Easy

CALORIES
199 kcal

INGREDIENTS

1/2 Cup Coconut Water

1/2 Cup Milk of Choice

1/4 Cup Papaya

1/4 Cup Pineapple

1/4 Tsp Ginger

1/2 Cup Ice

1 Tsp Collagen Powder

DIRECTIONS

1. Add all ingredients to a blender in the order listed.
2. Blend on high until smooth and creamy.
3. Taste and adjust sweetness or spiciness as needed.
4. Pour into a glass and enjoy immediately.

You can adjust the amount of ice to achieve your desired consistency. If you prefer a thicker smoothie, you can use less ice or add a frozen banana. The collagen powder is optional but adds protein and other health benefits to the smoothie.

NOTES

The orange color is filled with vitamin A but more so it also contains the color orange which in the chakra healing chart is great for the sacral chakra. This space is linked with creativity and enjoying the pleasures of life. Calories: 139

Total Fat: 2g. Saturated Fat: 1g. Trans Fat: 0g. Cholesterol: 0mg. Sodium: 79mg. Total Carbohydrates: 23g. Dietary Fiber: 2g

Sugars: 18g Protein: 7g. (You can add more collagen for more protein.)

Note: The nutrition facts may vary slightly depending on the specific brands and types of ingredients used. This smoothie is a good source of vitamin C, potassium, and protein from the collagen powder.

BOUJEE BERRY SMOOTHIE

FROZEN DRAGONS WITH BERRIES

Something about pink is so great for our wellness. We love pink fruits because colors are what make us feel great.

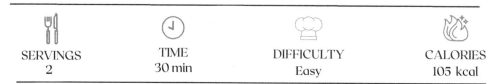

SERVINGS	TIME	DIFFICULTY	CALORIES
2	30 min	Easy	105 kcal

INGREDIENTS

1/2 cup dragon fruit

1/2 cup coconut water

1/2 cup almond milk

1/4 cup berries

1/4 cup ice

DIRECTIONS

1. Add the diced dragon fruit, mixed berries, and ice to a blender.
2. Pour in the coconut water and almond milk.
3. Blend the mixture until it is smooth and creamy.
4. Pour the smoothie into a glass and serve immediately.

Optional: You can add a sweetener of your choice, such as honey or agave syrup, to the smoothie for a sweeter taste. Enjoy your delicious and healthy Dragon Fruit Smoothie!

NOTES

Here are the approximate nutrition facts for one serving of Dragon Fruit Smoothie:

Calories: 105.   Total Fat: 2g.   Saturated Fat: 0g.   Trans Fat: 0g.   Cholesterol: 0mg

Sodium: 130mg.   Total Carbohydrates: 21g.   Dietary Fiber: 3g.   Sugars: 15g.   Protein: 2g

Please note that these values may vary depending on the specific brand of ingredients used and the exact measurements of each ingredient.

VANILLA SMOOTHIE

VANILLA BANANA SMOOTHIE

Vanilla Smoothies are so quick and easy to have in the morning for a creamy start to the day.

SERVINGS
2

TIME
30 min

DIFFICULTY
Easy

CALORIES
239 kcal

INGREDIENTS

350 ml Milk of choice

2 Frozen Bananas

2 Dates (optional)

1 Cup Ice

2 Tbs Vanilla Protein Powder (Optional)

DIRECTIONS

1. Peel the bananas and slice them into chunks. Freeze the banana chunks overnight or for at least 2 hours.
2. Add the frozen banana chunks, milk of your choice, and dates (if using) to a blender.
3. Blend the mixture until smooth and creamy.
4. Add the ice and protein powder (if using) to the blender and blend again until smooth.
5. Pour the smoothie into a glass and serve immediately.

Optional: You can add a sweetener of your choice, such as honey or maple syrup, to the smoothie for a sweeter taste.

Enjoy your delicious and healthy Banana Protein Smoothie!

NOTES

Banana smoothies are my favorite go to when I would like a filling yet somewhat decadent breakfast drink. When it comes to getting your vanilla flavor, this base is the best, you can choose vanilla collagen or a vanilla protein of choice. and you can add to it a 1/4 tsp maca powder for a hormone boost. Here are the approximate nutrition facts for one serving of Banana Protein Smoothie:

Calories: 354. Total Fat: 3g. Saturated Fat: 1g. Trans Fat: 0g. Cholesterol: 9mg. Sodium: 166mg. Total Carbohydrates: 68g. Dietary Fiber: 7g

Sugars: 43g. Protein: 18g. Please note that these values may vary depending on the specific brand of ingredients used and the exact measurements of each ingredient. The nutrition facts are calculated based on the use of almond milk, frozen bananas, no added sweetener, and whey protein powder.

RICE PORRIDGE

PORRIDGE

WARM COZY

Some mornings the body calls for a bowl of warm porridge. When it comes to getting cozy on a rainy day or taking it slow on the weekend, this recipe is one of my favorites. Double the recipe if you are having guests.

SERVINGS	TIME	DIFFICULTY	CALORIES
1	30 min	Easy	150 kcal

INGREDIENTS

1 4 cup raw Bob's red mill rice farina

½ tsp ground clove

1 cinnamon stick or ½ tsp cinnamon

¾- 1 cup almond milk (optional) or water

1 tbsp. sweetener of choice

1 handful raspberries (frozen or raw)

1 pinch of salt

DIRECTIONS

1. In a small saucepan, combine the rice farina, ground clove, and cinnamon stick or ground cinnamon.
2. Add 3/4 cup of almond milk or water to the pan, along with a pinch of salt.
3. Stir the mixture well to combine the ingredients.
4. Bring the mixture to a boil over medium heat, stirring occasionally.
5. Once the mixture reaches a boil, reduce the heat to low and let it simmer for 5-7 minutes, or until the rice farina has cooked through and the porridge has thickened to your liking.
6. Remove the cinnamon stick (if using) from the pan.
7. Stir in 1 tablespoon of sweetener of your choice.
8. Add the raspberries to the pan and stir gently to combine. The raspberries will soften and release their juices, adding a natural sweetness and beautiful color to the porridge.
9. If the porridge is too thick for your liking, add a splash of almond milk or water to thin it out to your desired consistency.
10. Serve the warm porridge in a bowl and enjoy!

NOTES

My fondest memories of porridge take me back to primary school. Having breakfast served and enjoying a yummy bowl of milky porridge was a favorite. Only in my late twenties did I rekindle my love for porridge when I found rice porridge after going gluten free. You can sub out the rice porridge for oats if you prefer. You can remove spices if you don't like them and sweeten to taste. Here are the estimated nutrition facts for one serving of the rice farina porridge recipe:

Calories: 200 Total Fat: 3g Saturated Fat: 0.3g Trans Fat: 0g Cholesterol: 0mg Sodium: 80mg Total Carbohydrates: 39g Dietary Fiber: 4g Sugars: 11g Protein: 4g

Please note that these values may vary depending on the specific brand of ingredients used and the exact measurements of each ingredient. The nutrition facts are calculated based on the use of almond milk and honey as the sweetener.

CHIA PUDDING

Ingredients

2 cups unsweetened almond milk
1/2 cup chia seeds
2 tbsp sweetener of choice (e.g. honey, maple syrup, agave nectar)
1/4 tsp salt
11/2 tsp vanilla extract
2 cups fresh or frozen berries (e.g. strawberries, blueberries, raspberries)

2 cups of awesome
1/2 tsp of fun
3 tbsp color
1 cup of kindness
salt and pepper to taste

Directions

1 In a large bowl, whisk together the almond milk, chia seeds, sweetener of choice, salt, and vanilla extract until well combined.

2 Cover the bowl with plastic wrap or a lid and refrigerate for at least 4 hours or overnight. The chia seeds will absorb the liquid and the mixture will thicken into a pudding-like consistency.

3 Once the chia seed pudding has thickened, give it a good stir to make sure there are no clumps of chia seeds.

4 To serve, divide the chia seed pudding evenly among 4 serving dishes or jars.

5 Top each serving with a generous amount of fresh or frozen berries.

6 Drizzle additional sweetener of your choice over the top of each serving, if desired.

7 Serve immediately and enjoy!

Chia puddings are great for meal prep and for adding some sweetness to your life. This chia seed pudding can be stored in the refrigerator for up to 5 days, so it's a great make-ahead breakfast or snack.

You can also experiment with different toppings, such as chopped nuts, coconut flakes, or granola, to add texture and flavor.

Optional: You can add toppings of your choice, such as nuts, seeds, or additional fruit.
Enjoy your delicious and nutritious Berry Chia Seed Pudding. Calories: 220. Total Fat: 10g. Saturated Fat: 1g Trans Fat: 0g.
Cholesterol: 0mg. Sodium: 170mg. Total Carbohydrates: 29g Dietary Fiber: 14g. Sugars: 9g. Protein: 7g

Please note that these nutrition facts are estimates and may vary based on the specific ingredients and brands used. Additionally, if you modify the recipe by using a different sweetener or milk, the nutrition information will be different.

CASSAVA CREPES GF

Gluten-free crepes are fantastic to add to the meal plan for any given week or month. Great for a brunch for one or breakfast for the whole family. Crepes are one of my favorite go-to's because they are easy to make and so filling. I love having them sweet with honey when my sweet tooth calls but I also love enjoying them as part of a savory meal also. My mom introduced me to crepes during our travels in my early childhood years in Martinique.

SERVINGS	TIME	DIFFICULTY	CALORIES
2	30 min	Easy	268 kcal

INGREDIENTS

1/3 cup Carmeta's Pancake Mix

1 Eggs

1 tsp Vanilla

3/4 Cup Water

3 tbsp Butter or oil

DIRECTIONS

1. In a large mixing bowl, whisk together the Carmeta's Pancake Mix, egg, vanilla extract, and water until well combined and no lumps remain.
2. In a large skillet or griddle, heat the butter or oil over medium-high heat until melted and hot.
3. Pour 1/4 cup of the pancake batter onto the skillet or griddle for each pancake, leaving space between them.
4. Cook the pancakes until the edges begin to dry and the bottom is golden brown, about 2-3 minutes.
5. Flip the pancakes and cook until the other side is golden brown, about 1-2 minutes more.
6. Repeat with the remaining batter, adding more butter or oil to the skillet as needed.

Serve the pancakes hot with your favorite toppings, such as fresh berries, syrup, whipped cream, or butter. Enjoy your delicious and easy Carmetta's Pancake Mix pancakes!

NOTES

Here are the approximate nutrition facts for one serving of these Carmeta's Pancake Mix pancakes: Calories: 268. Total Fat: 17g. Saturated Fat: 7g. Trans Fat: 0g

Cholesterol: 91mg. Sodium: 297mg Total Carbohydrates: 22g Dietary Fiber: 1g. Sugars: 1g

Protein: 6g. Please note that these values may vary depending on the specific brand of ingredients used and the exact measurements of each ingredient. Additionally, the nutrition facts may change depending on the amount of butter or oil used for cooking the pancakes.

AVOCADO TOAST

AVOCADOS WITH SPICES

Avocados on toast are one of the best combos for sure. With a sprinkle of chili flakes and on a sourdough toast, this is certainly a breakfast favorite. Note: You can adjust the amount of spices to your liking, and you can also add other toppings to the avocado toast, such as sliced tomatoes, red onions, or a poached egg. This recipe makes 2 servings.

SERVINGS	TIME	DIFFICULTY	CALORIES
2	5-7 min	Easy	286 kcal

INGREDIENTS

2 slices of sourdough

1 avocado

1 sprinkle pink salt

1 dash black pepper

1 sprinkle chili flakes
(optional)

DIRECTIONS

1. Toast the sourdough bread slices in a toaster or on a grill until crispy and golden brown.
2. While the bread is toasting, scoop out the avocado flesh into a small bowl.
3. Add the pink salt and black pepper to the avocado, and mash it with a fork until it reaches your desired texture.
4. Once the bread is toasted, spread the mashed avocado evenly on top of each slice.
5. Sprinkle chili flakes on top of the avocado (optional).
6. Serve the avocado toast immediately, while it's still warm and crispy.

NOTES

Here are the estimated nutrition facts for one serving of the Avocado Toast with Sourdough and Spices recipe: Calories: 286 Total Fat: 16.4g. Saturated Fat: 2.4g Trans Fat: 0g. Cholesterol: 0mg. Sodium: 311mg. Total Carbohydrates: 27.6g. Dietary Fiber: 10.4g
Sugars: 2g. Protein: 8g. Note: The nutrition facts may vary slightly depending on the specific type and amount of bread used, and the amount of spices added. Avocado toast is a good source of healthy fats, fiber, and protein.

OMELET WITH HERBS

Omelets take a few key notes to get it just right including having the right pan, the right temperature, cooking technique, and the flipping of the pie to ensure well cooked all the way through but still fluffy and soft on the inside.

SERVINGS	TIME	DIFFICULTY	CALORIES
2	10-15 min	Easy	242 kcal

INGREDIENTS

2 Scrambled Eggs

1 Diced Tomato

1/4 Cup Mushroom

1 Handful Chopped Spinach

3 Stalks Chopped Parsley or Chives

Pinch Salt

Sprinkle Black pepper

DIRECTIONS

1. Crack the eggs into a bowl and whisk them together until well combined.
2. Heat a non-stick skillet over medium heat.
3. Melt the butter or oil in the skillet.
4. Add the diced tomato and sliced mushrooms to the skillet and sauté for 2-3 minutes until the vegetables are soft and fragrant.
5. Add the chopped spinach to the skillet and stir until the spinach has wilted, about 1-2 minutes.
6. Pour the beaten eggs over the vegetables and let the eggs cook for 1-2 minutes.
7. Use a spatula to lift the edges of the omelette and allow any uncooked egg to flow underneath.
8. Once the eggs are mostly set, add a pinch of salt and a sprinkle of black pepper to taste.
9. Fold the omelette in half and cook for an additional 1-2 minutes until the eggs are fully cooked.
10. Top the omelet with the chopped herbs and serve hot.

NOTES

Sometimes I make omelets plain and thin and separately cook the veggies and fold them in separately. If I mess it up, I end up scrambling the omelet so don't be upset if it doesn't turn out perfect the first try. You can try again until you find the style that works for you and mix it up also so you don't get bored. Here are the approximate nutrition facts for the omelette recipe:

Calories: 242 Total fat: 18g. Saturated fat: 7g Trans fat: 0g. Cholesterol: 384mg. Sodium: 268mg

Total carbohydrates: 7g. Dietary fiber: 2g. Sugars: 3g. Protein: 14g

PLANTAINS WITH HONEY

Ripe plantains are one of my absolute favorite monthly purchases. They are great baked or air fried to reduce fat calories compared to pan frying. I like them sliced thinner to be crispier.

SERVINGS	TIME	DIFFICULTY	CALORIES
4	30 min	Easy	218 kcal

INGREDIENTS

4 Ripe Plantains

2 Tsp Honey

1 Pinch Cinnamon

DIRECTIONS

1. Preheat the oven to 400°F (200°C). Slice plantains in thin slices on a slight diagonal.
2. Peel the plantains and cut them into 1-inch thick slices.
3. Arrange the plantain slices in a single layer on a baking sheet lined with parchment paper.
4. Drizzle the honey over the plantains, making sure each slice is coated.
5. Sprinkle the cinnamon over the plantains.
6. Bake the plantains in the preheated oven for 20-25 minutes or until golden brown and tender.
7. Remove from the oven and let cool for a few minutes before serving.

NOTES

Baked plantains are my favorite secret sweet treat. When I want to start my day with a sweet treat or add something natural to brunch, I choose plantains. I enjoy them for a side in a Caribbean Full Breakfast but also as a main itself. Sometimes for a quick option, I choose already prepared and frozen plantains. Calories: 200. Total fat: 0.5g. Saturated fat: 0g Trans fat: 0g Cholesterol: 0mg. Sodium: 1mg Total carbohydrates: 53g Dietary fiber: 3g Sugars: 25g. Protein: 2g

BREAKFAST SANDWICH

I love a breakfast sandwich to fuel up a healthy day. Morning fuel keeps us steady so that we can keep productive and profitable.

SERVINGS	TIME	DIFFICULTY	CALORIES
2	30 min	Easy	236 kcal

INGREDIENTS

2 Fried Eggs

2 Glutenfree or Sourdough Toast

1 Tbsp Olive Oil

1/4 Cup Mushrooms

Ketchup if desired

DIRECTIONS

1. Preheat a non-stick skillet over medium-high heat. Add 1 tablespoon of olive oil.
2. Add the sliced mushrooms to the skillet and sauté until tender, about 3-4 minutes. Season with salt and pepper to taste.
3. Remove the mushrooms from the skillet and set aside.
4. Crack the eggs into the skillet and cook to your desired level of doneness (sunny side up, over easy, etc.).
5. While the eggs are cooking, toast the gluten-free bread slices.
6. Once the eggs are done, remove them from the skillet and assemble the breakfast by placing the eggs on top of the toasted bread slices, and spooning the sautéed mushrooms over the top.
7. Serve with ketchup on the side (if desired).

Enjoy your delicious and nutritious breakfast with fried eggs, mushrooms, and gluten-free toast!

NOTES

A breakfast sandwich is one of my favorite meals to have during the week that is quick to make and easy to assemble. Here are the approximate nutrition facts for this recipe:
Calories: 420 Total fat: 25g Saturated fat: 5g Trans fat: 0g Cholesterol: 370mg Sodium: 520mg Total carbohydrates: 25g Dietary fiber: 3g Sugars: 2g Protein: 21g Please note that the nutrition facts may vary slightly depending on the specific brands and ingredients used.

WATERMELON LOLLY

Staying cool during the heat waves is essential. When it comes to an ice-cold lolly, nothing beats that on a hot day.

SERVINGS 2	TIME 30 min	DIFFICULTY Easy	CALORIES 30 kcal

INGREDIENTS

1 small water melon

fruit

Lolly sticks

NOTES

DIRECTIONS

1. Cut up fruit in triangles.
2. Assemble on a lolly stick.

Alternatively
1. Cut the watermelon into small pieces and remove any seeds.
2. Place the watermelon pieces into a blender and blend until smooth.
3. Pour the watermelon puree into lolly molds, filling them about 3/4 of the way full.
4. Insert the lolly sticks into the molds.
5. Place the lolly molds in the freezer for at least 4 hours, or until the lollies are completely frozen.
6. Once the lollies are frozen, remove them from the molds by running them under hot water for a few seconds.
7. Serve and enjoy!

These watermelon lollies are not only delicious and refreshing, but they are also a healthy alternative to sugary snacks.
Here are the approximate nutrition facts for these watermelon lollies: Serving size: 1 lolly Calories: 30 Total fat: 0.1g
Cholesterol: 0mg Sodium: 1mg. Total carbohydrates: 8g Dietary fiber: 0.6g Sugars: 6.2g Protein: 0.6g
Please note that the nutrition facts may vary slightly depending on the specific size and amount of watermelon used, as well as any additional sweeteners or flavorings.

CHICKEN WRAP
WITH HUMMUS

I love chicken wraps because they are quick to assemble, taste good, and recharge the batteries.

SERVINGS	TIME	DIFFICULTY	CALORIES
1	10-15 min	Easy	330-400 kcal

INGREDIENTS

3 oz cooked chicken, sliced or shredded

1 wrap

1 tbsp hummus

1 spoonful pesto

1 handful of lettuce

1/2 tomato, sliced

DIRECTIONS

1. Lay the wrap flat on a clean surface.
2. Spread the hummus evenly on the wrap.
3. Add the pesto on top of the hummus and spread it evenly.
4. Place the lettuce on top of the pesto.
5. Add the sliced chicken on top of the lettuce.
6. Place the sliced tomatoes on top of the chicken.
7. Fold the bottom of the wrap up to cover the ingredients.
8. Fold the sides of the wrap inwards towards the center.
9. Roll the wrap upwards until it is completely closed.
10. Cut the wrap in half, if desired, and serve.

Enjoy your delicious chicken wrap with hummus and pesto!

NOTES

You can add or remove sauces as you wish. I like a gluten-free wrap. The nutrition facts for this recipe may vary depending on the specific ingredients used and the size of the wrap. Here is a general estimate based on the ingredients listed: Calories: 330-400 Protein: 25-30 grams Fat: 13-17 grams Carbohydrates: 25-35 grams Fiber: 4-6 grams Sugar: 3-5 grams Sodium: 350-450 milligrams . Please note that these nutrition facts are approximate and may vary depending on the specific ingredients and brands used.

CARIBBEAN BRUNCH

There are many cultures that have staple breakfasts which I do enjoy like an English breakfast or French pastries from time to time, but this combination I feel defines the exact experience of The Caribbean Breakfast relative to a menu choice. The nutrition facts may vary depending on the exact ingredients used and the serving size, but this recipe is generally high in protein, healthy fats, fiber, vitamins, and minerals. It's a great breakfast option for those who follow a gluten-free, dairy-free, or paleo diet.

SERVINGS
4

TIME
30 min

DIFFICULTY
Easy

CALORIES
420 kcal

INGREDIENTS

2 Plantains, peeled and sliced

1 Cup Mushrooms sliced thinly

½ Avocado sliced finely

1 tomato sliced

6-8 Eggs

2 gluten free slices toast

4 tbsp. olive oil

Sea Salt to taste

Black pepper to taste

Chives to garnish

DIRECTIONS

1. Heat 2 tbsp of olive oil in a skillet over medium heat. Add sliced plantains and cook for 3-4 minutes on each side or until golden brown. Remove from skillet and set aside.
2. In the same skillet, add 1 tbsp of olive oil and sliced mushrooms. Cook for 5-6 minutes or until tender. Season with salt and pepper to taste. Remove from skillet and set aside.
3. In the same skillet, add 1 tbsp of olive oil and crack the eggs in. Cook the eggs to your desired doneness. Season with salt and pepper to taste.
4. Toast the gluten-free bread.
5. On a plate, assemble the dish by placing the toasted bread at the bottom, followed by the cooked plantains, mushrooms, sliced avocado, and sliced tomato.
6. Top with the fried eggs and garnish with chives.
7. Serve and enjoy your delicious and nutritious breakfast!

To assemble, add your avocado to your toast and plate up your plantain, mushrooms, and tomato for a simple Caribbean-styled breakfast/ brunch.

NOTES

When it comes to putting a group of ingredients together for an acquired taste experience, it is interesting how the palette loves certain flavors. If you feel to add another protein source my recommendations include smoked fish of choice.
Note: You can also add some hot sauce or salsa for extra flavor if desired.

The total calorie count for the ingredients in the recipe would depend on the specific quantities used, but here is an estimate based on average serving sizes: 2 plantains: 320 calories 1 cup mushrooms: 15 calories ½ avocado: 160 calories 1 tomato: 22 calories
6-8 eggs: 468-624 calories. 2 gluten-free toast: 200 calories 4 tbsp. olive oil: 480 calories Sea salt and black pepper: negligible calories
Chives: negligible calories Total calories: approximately 1665-1821 calories

BRUNCH CHARCUTERIE

FRIENDLY FUN

These are so much fun to assemble for small plates with friends when focusing on portions especially.

SERVINGS	TIME	DIFFICULTY	CALORIES
4	30 min	Easy	290-520 kcal

INGREDIENTS

1 cup grapes

1 cup strawberries

4 oz sausages, sliced

4 oz soft goat cheese

4 oz brie cheese

8-10 gluten-free crackers

2 tbsp capers

1/4 cup mixed olives

4 oz smoked salmon, sliced

1 cup baby carrots

DIRECTIONS

1. Arrange a large platter or board.
2. Place the goat cheese and brie cheese on the board.
3. Add the sliced sausages, smoked salmon, and capers.
4. Place the gluten-free crackers around the board.
5. Add the grapes, carrots and strawberries.
6. While they are in the oven, I chop up all the mushrooms, and tomatoes and slice the avocado into slices after peeling back the skin.
7. Scatter the mixed olives around the board.
8. Serve and enjoy!

NOTES

Charcuterie boards are a great idea when having friends over for small bites while catching up. Throw in some bloody marys and mimosas and you have a party. Recommended portions: 1-2 oz of cheese per person, 2-3 slices of sausage per person, 1-2 oz of smoked salmon per person. 1/4-1/2 cup of grapes and strawberries per person, 1-2 gluten-free crackers per person 1-2 tbsp of capers and mixed olives per person. Total calorie range per serving: 290-520 calories. Please note that this is an estimate and may vary depending on the exact brands and types of ingredients used. Here are the macronutrient figures for one serving of the charcuterie board:
Calories: 271 Protein: 15g Fat: 19g Carbohydrates: 12g Fiber: 2g Sugar: 7g

GORGEOUS GREENS

SALADS

FUEL YOUR MIND AND BODY

SUMMER SALAD

When it comes to keeping hydrated, there is nothing like a refreshing salad to do the job.

SERVINGS	TIME	DIFFICULTY	CALORIES
2	30 min	Easy	126 kcal

INGREDIENTS

4 cups of your favorite salad greens (such as spinach, arugula, or mixed greens)
1 cup of cooked and sliced vegetables (such as roasted sweet potatoes, grilled zucchini, or sautéed mushrooms)

For the dressing:
1 lemon, juiced
2 tablespoons of olive oil
1 tablespoon of Dijon mustard
1 tablespoon of honey
1 pinch of salt
1 pinch of black pepper
2 dashes of Italian herb seasoning

DIRECTIONS

1. Begin by washing and drying your salad greens, then placing them in a large bowl.
2. Add the cooked and sliced vegetables to the bowl with the greens.
3. In a small mixing bowl, whisk together the lemon juice, olive oil, Dijon mustard, honey, salt, black pepper, and Italian herb seasoning until well combined.
4. Drizzle the dressing over the salad, tossing everything together to ensure that the dressing is evenly distributed.
5. Serve the salad immediately, garnished with additional herbs or toppings of your choice, if desired.

NOTES

I love this salad as a staple base in all of my salads pretty much. I then proceed to add any additional toppings which could range from grilled protein, or gluten free pasta depending on the day. Based on the recipe above, here is the nutrition information for a single serving (assuming four servings in total):
Serving Size: 1/4 of the recipe Calories: 126 Total Fat: 9g Saturated Fat: 1g Trans Fat: 0g Cholesterol: 0mg
Sodium: 137mg Total Carbohydrates: 11g Dietary Fiber: 2g Sugars: 8g Protein: 2g

LETTUCE WRAPS

I love these with Mexican style chicken on a day when the body wants something light and delicious.

SERVINGS	TIME	DIFFICULTY	CALORIES
2	30 min	Easy	190 kcal

INGREDIENTS

2 chicken breasts, diced

3 garlic cloves, minced

1/2 green pepper, diced

1/2 yellow pepper, diced

1 onion, largely diced

2 pimentos, minced

4 shadow beni leaves, finely chopped

2 tablespoons of paprika

2 tablespoons of tomato paste

3 tablespoons of chopped cilantro or shadow beni

3 tomatoes, diced

2 sprigs of chives, chopped

1 lime, cut into wedges

1 lemon, juiced

2 teaspoons of chicken seasoning or allspice

Salt and pepper to taste

Lettuce leaves for wrapping

DIRECTIONS

1. In a large skillet, heat some oil over medium heat. Add the chicken and cook until it's no longer pink, stirring occasionally. Remove the chicken from the skillet and set it aside.

2. In the same skillet, sauté the garlic, onion, and peppers until they're soft and fragrant. Add the pimentos and shadow beni leaves and cook for another 2 minutes.

3. Return the cooked chicken to the skillet, and add the paprika, tomato paste, chicken seasoning, and salt and pepper to taste. Stir to combine and cook for another 5-7 minutes until everything is heated through and the flavors have melded together.

4. Remove the skillet from heat and add the chopped cilantro or shadow beni, chopped chives, and diced tomatoes. Mix well.

5. To serve, spoon the chicken mixture onto lettuce leaves and roll them up like a wrap. Squeeze some fresh lime juice over the top and enjoy!

6. This recipe makes approximately 6-8 lettuce wraps. Enjoy!

NOTES

Mexican chicken is one of my favorites on my meal prep list and sometimes a light lettuce wrap cup is a great way to share with friends or have an easy week day dinner. Serving Size: 1/6 of the recipe Calories: 190 Total Fat: 4g Saturated Fat: 1g Trans Fat: 0g Cholesterol: 60mg Sodium: 410mg Total Carbohydrates: 14g Dietary Fiber: 4g Sugars: 6g Protein: 24g

It's important to note that the nutrition information may vary based on the specific brands of ingredients used, as well as the type and amount of lettuce used for wrapping. However, this gives you a general idea of the nutritional breakdown of the chicken lettuce wraps.

COLESLAW

This is one of my favorite recipes ever. I love this side salad, particularly with roasted chicken and roasted vegetables.

SERVINGS	TIME	DIFFICULTY	CALORIES
2	30 min	Easy	95 kcal

INGREDIENTS

3 cups shredded red and green cabbage

2 green onions, sliced

1/4 cup mayonnaise or vegan mayonnaise

Handful of chopped cilantro

2 tablespoons lime juice

Salt and pepper to taste

DIRECTIONS

1. In a large mixing bowl, combine the shredded red and green cabbage and sliced green onions.
2. In a separate small mixing bowl, whisk together the mayonnaise or vegan mayonnaise, chopped cilantro, lime juice, and salt and pepper to taste.
3. Pour the dressing over the cabbage mixture and toss to combine, making sure all of the cabbage is coated in the dressing.
4. Taste the coleslaw and adjust the seasoning as needed.
5. Chill the coleslaw in the refrigerator for at least 30 minutes before serving to allow the flavors to meld together.
6. This coleslaw recipe is perfect for serving as a side dish for burgers, sandwiches, or any other summer meal. Enjoy!

NOTES

There is always room for great habits. Salads are one of my favorite items to have as part of my routine. This recipes is one that I enjoy after a long work day with warm roasted proteins or as part of a social friendly gathering. The nutrition information for this coleslaw recipe will vary based on the specific brand of ingredients used, but here is the approximate nutritional information for a single serving of coleslaw (assuming four servings in total): Serving Size: 1/4 of the recipe Calories: 95 Total Fat: 8g Saturated Fat: 1g Trans Fat: 0g Cholesterol: 5mg Sodium: 115mg Total Carbohydrates: 6g Dietary Fiber: 2g Sugars: 3g Protein: 1g

SPRING SALAD

Refreshing

SERVINGS	TIME	DIFFICULTY	CALORIES
2	10 min	Easy	358 kcal

INGREDIENTS

4 dried figs, thinly sliced

4 cups lettuce, chopped or Arugala

1 carrot, peeled and grated

1 tsp sesame seeds

2 tsp goat feta, crumbled

For the Lemon Dijon Dressing:

1 lemon, juiced

1 tsp dijon mustard

1 tsp honey

1 tbsp olive oil

1 tsp dried oregano

1-2 turns cracked black pepper

2 turns of cracked sea salt

DIRECTIONS

1. Start by preparing the Lemon Dijon Dressing. In a small bowl, whisk together the lemon juice, dijon mustard, honey, olive oil, dried oregano, black pepper, and sea salt until well combined.
2. In a large mixing bowl, add the chopped lettuce and grated carrot. Pour the Lemon Dijon Dressing over the top and toss to combine, making sure all of the veggies are coated in the dressing.
3. Divide the dressed lettuce and carrot mixture between 2-4 plates, depending on the desired serving size.
4. Sprinkle the thinly sliced dried figs, sesame seeds, and crumbled goat feta over the top of each salad.
5. Serve immediately and enjoy!

NOTES

The nutrition information for this salad recipe will vary based on the specific brand of ingredients used, but here is the approximate nutritional information for a single serving of salad (assuming four servings in total): Serving Size: 1/4 of the recipe. Calories: 120 Total Fat: 8g Saturated Fat: 2g Trans Fat: 0g Cholesterol: 5mg Sodium: 220mg Total Carbohydrates: 11g Dietary Fiber: 2g Sugars: 7g Protein: 2g

GRILLED CHICKEN SALAD

Chicken Salads are hands down one of my all time favourite meals.

SERVINGS
2

TIME
30 min

DIFFICULTY
Easy

CALORIES
400 kcal

INGREDIENTS

1/2 tsp salt

1/2 tsp black pepper

1/2 tsp ground cumin

1/2 tsp chili powder

1/2 tsp garlic powder

1/2 tsp onion powder

1 pound boneless, skinless chicken breasts

4 cups mixed greens, chopped

Optional toppings: cherry tomatoes, sliced avocado, diced red onion, shredded cheese, croutons

DIRECTIONS

1. Preheat grill or grill pan over medium-high heat.
2. In a small bowl, mix together the salt, black pepper, ground cumin, chili powder, garlic powder, and onion powder.
3. Rub the spice mixture over both sides of the chicken breasts.
4. Grill the chicken for 6-8 minutes per side, or until cooked through and no longer pink in the middle.
5. Remove the chicken from the grill and let it rest for 5 minutes before slicing it into thin strips.
6. In a large bowl, add the chopped mixed greens and toss with your desired amount of dressing.
7. Top the greens with the sliced grilled chicken and any optional toppings you desire.
8. Serve immediately and enjoy!

NOTES

No time to cook? Purchase a rotisserie chicken to add as your protein to your salad. You can sub out canned tuna, mackerel, tuna, salmon, or hard boiled eggs. The nutrition information for this salad recipe will vary based on the specific brand of ingredients used, but here is the approximate nutritional information for a single serving of salad (assuming four servings in total):

Serving Size: 1/4 of the recipe Calories: 200 Total Fat: 6g Saturated Fat: 1g Trans Fat: 0g Cholesterol: 75mg Sodium: 400mg Total Carbohydrates: 6g Dietary Fiber: 2g Sugars: 2g Protein: 30g

POKE BOWL
WITH SUSHI RICE

This is one of my favorite bowls when it comes to comfort food.

SERVINGS	TIME	DIFFICULTY	CALORIES
2	30 min	Easy	450 kcal

INGREDIENTS

3/4 lb of tuna, cut into small cubes

3 sprigs of spring onion, thinly sliced

1 cup sushi rice

1 tbsp sesame oil

2 tbsp rice vinegar

2 tbsp soy sauce

1 tbsp sesame seeds

1 tbsp peanut butter

2 tbsp honey or sugar

1 cucumber, sliced

1 carrot, shredded

1/2 cup avocado, sliced

2 cups greens Salad

2 Sheets nori, cut into thin strips

DIRECTIONS

1. Rinse the sushi rice in cold water until the water runs clear. Cook the rice according to package instructions.
2. In a small bowl, whisk together the sesame oil, rice vinegar, soy sauce, sesame seeds, peanut butter, and honey (or sugar) to make the dressing.
3. In a large bowl, combine the cooked sushi rice, tuna cubes, sliced spring onions, and dressing. Mix well to combine.
4. Divide the rice and tuna mixture among four bowls.
5. Top each bowl with sliced cucumber, shredded carrot, sliced avocado, and a handful of greens salad.
6. Garnish each bowl with strips of nori and serve immediately.
7. Note: The nutrition information for this poke bowl recipe will vary based on the specific brand of ingredients used, but here is the approximate nutritional information for a single serving of poke bowl (assuming four servings in total):

NOTES

Poke bowl salads remind me of a deconstructed sushi roll and is certainly one of my very favorite meals. Serving Size: 1/4 of the recipe Calories: 450 Total Fat: 16g Saturated Fat: 3g

Trans Fat: 0g Cholesterol: 50mg Sodium: 650mg Total Carbohydrates: 47g Dietary Fiber: 5g

Sugars: 13g Protein: 30g

LEAN COZY SOUPS

COMFORT
FUEL YOUR MIND AND BODY
IN A BOWL

CAULIFLOWER SOUP

This is one of my favorite soups ever. I love soup and this by far suits my creamy soup cravings and it is dairy free which is the best feeling for the heart and the stomach.

SERVINGS	TIME	DIFFICULTY	CALORIES
2	30 min	Easy	120 kcal

INGREDIENTS

1 tsp oil or butter

1 head cauliflower, chopped into florets

2 cups broth (vegetable or chicken)

1 cup vegan cream of mushroom soup

3 tbsp chives, chopped

Paprika, salt, and pepper to taste

Dairy-free milk (optional, for added creaminess)

1 stock cube (optional, for added flavor)

DIRECTIONS

1. In a large pot, heat the oil or butter over medium-high heat. Add the cauliflower florets and cook for 5-7 minutes, stirring occasionally, until lightly browned.
2. Add the broth and stock cube (if using) to the pot and bring to a boil. Reduce the heat and simmer for 15-20 minutes, or until the cauliflower is tender.
3. Use an immersion blender or transfer the soup to a blender and blend until smooth.
4. Add the vegan cream of mushroom soup, chives, and paprika, salt, and pepper to taste. Stir to combine.
5. If you want the soup to be even creamier, add a splash of dairy-free milk and stir to combine.
6. Serve hot, garnished with extra chives and paprika, if desired.

NOTES

Creamy cauliflower soup is one of my favorite meals ever. I love it on an evening for movies or sitting for an outdoor meal with a rad playlist. Note: The nutritional information for this soup will vary based on the specific brands of ingredients used, but here is the approximate nutritional information per serving (assuming four servings in total): Serving Size: 1/4 of the recipe Calories: 120 Total Fat: 5g Saturated Fat: 1g Trans Fat: 0g Cholesterol: 0mg Sodium: 1000mg Total Carbohydrates: 17g Dietary Fiber: 4g Sugars: 7g Protein: 4g

PUMPKIN SOUP

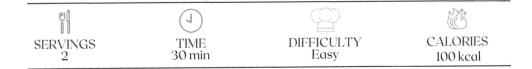

This is my ultimate go to for glowing skin and for a light and hearty meal

SERVINGS	TIME	DIFFICULTY	CALORIES
2	30 min	Easy	100 kcal

INGREDIENTS

1 small pumpkin, peeled and cubed

1 small squash, peeled and cubed

2 cups chicken broth

1 cup almond milk

1 tsp paprika

Salt and pepper to taste

DIRECTIONS

1. In a large pot, combine the pumpkin, squash, and chicken broth. Bring to a boil and then reduce heat to medium-low. Simmer for about 20 minutes or until the pumpkin and squash are tender.
2. Using an immersion blender or transferring the mixture to a blender, blend the soup until smooth.
3. Add the almond milk, paprika, salt, and pepper to the pot and stir until combined. Simmer for an additional 5-10 minutes, stirring occasionally.
4. Adjust the seasoning as necessary and serve hot.
5. Enjoy your creamy and flavorful Pumpkin and Squash Soup!

NOTES

Note: The nutritional information for this soup will vary based on the specific brands of ingredients used, but here is the approximate nutritional information per serving (assuming 4 servings in total): Serving Size: 1 cup Calories: 100 Total Fat: 2g Saturated Fat: 0g Trans Fat: 0g Cholesterol: 0mg Sodium: 400mg Total Carbohydrates: 21g Dietary Fiber: 4g Sugars: 7g Protein: 4g

CHICKEN BROTH

Broth is one of my monthly go-tos and my favorite to have around the house.

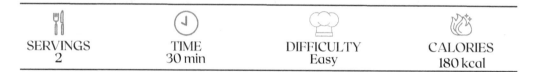

SERVINGS	TIME	DIFFICULTY	CALORIES
2	30 min	Easy	180 kcal

INGREDIENTS

900g chicken with bone

4 celery sticks, chopped

1 large onion, finely chopped

2 garlic cloves, minced

1 large carrot, peeled and chopped

2 tablespoons chopped parsley

2 teaspoons thyme

8 cups water

1/2 teaspoon black pepper

1 teaspoon paprika

1 teaspoon sage

1/2 sweet potato, peeled and chopped

DIRECTIONS

1. In a large pot, add the chicken, celery, onion, garlic, carrot, parsley, thyme, and water. Bring to a boil and then reduce heat to low. Simmer for 1-2 hours or until the chicken is fully cooked and tender.

2. Remove the chicken from the pot and let it cool for a few minutes. Once cool, remove the bones and shred the chicken meat.

3. Add the shredded chicken meat back into the pot along with the black pepper, paprika, sage, and sweet potato. Stir to combine and let the soup simmer for an additional 20-30 minutes or until the sweet potato is fully cooked and tender.

4. Serve hot and enjoy your delicious and comforting chicken soup!

NOTES

This is a crowd-pleaser. This is certainly one of the best chicken soups ever and one of my favorites to keep and stock up in batches. Serving Size: 1 cup Calories: 180 Total Fat: 8g Saturated Fat: 2g Trans Fat: 0g Cholesterol: 70mg Sodium: 170mg Total Carbohydrates: 6g Dietary Fiber: 1g Sugars: 2g Protein: 22g

CARROT SOUP
WITH SPICES

Carrot soup is one of those delicious light soups to make at the end of the week with leftovers or to have early on the week as a light lunch.

SERVINGS	TIME	DIFFICULTY	CALORIES
2	30 min	Easy	220 kcal/ serving

INGREDIENTS

1 tablespoon butter/ oil

½ tsp turmeric

1 small onion, diced

1 dash cumin

1 tsp ginger finely chopped

5-7 oz. chicken pieces (optional)

1-2 large sweet potatoes cut into
large chunks

5 carrots diced

2 cloves garlic

2 cups chicken stock, vegetable
stock, bean stock, or water (NO msg)

Fresh parsley

DIRECTIONS

1. In a large pot or Dutch oven, heat the butter or oil over medium heat.
2. Add the turmeric, onion, cumin, and ginger to the pot and stir to combine.
3. Cook for 3-4 minutes until the onion is soft and translucent.
4. Add the chicken pieces (if using) and cook until browned on all sides.
5. Add the sweet potatoes, carrots, and garlic to the pot and stir to combine.
6. Pour in the chicken stock or water and bring to a boil.
7. Reduce the heat to low and simmer for 25-30 minutes, until the vegetables are tender and the chicken is cooked through (if using).
8. Remove the pot from the heat and allow to cool slightly.
9. Use an immersion blender or transfer the soup to a blender and blend until smooth.
10. Return the soup to the pot and heat over low heat.
11. Add salt and pepper to taste.
12. Serve the soup hot, garnished with fresh parsley.

NOTES

Soups are always a good idea to make and keep in the freezer when you have ingredients that you may think you will get anxious if you don't use in time. Here are the approximate nutrition facts for one serving size of 1.5 cups of the recipe: Calories: 220 Total Fat: 9g Saturated Fat: 3g Trans Fat: 0g Cholesterol: 30mg Sodium: 390mg Total Carbohydrates: 27g Dietary Fiber: 6g Sugars: 8g Protein: 10g Note: These nutrition facts are approximate and may vary depending on the exact ingredients and quantities used.

VEGAN CREAM OF MUSHROOM

SOUP

This soup is a classic favourite.

SERVINGS 3-5	TIME 30 min	DIFFICULTY Easy	CALORIES 164 kcal

INGREDIENTS

1 tbsp. olive oil

1 onion, diced

2 tsp crushed garlic

1 tsp dried oregano

2 tsp calypso chicken dried spice seasoning

2 packs (500g/18oz) mushrooms of choice, sliced

1 pack (250g/ 9 oz) brown button mushrooms (portobellini), sliced

2 large Portobello mushrooms, sliced

2 tbsp. soy sauce/tamari or coconut aminos

1 cup coconut milk

1 cup unsweetened original almond milk

2 cups chicken bone broth

Sea salt to taste

Black pepper to taste

NOTES

DIRECTIONS

1. In a large pot, heat the olive oil over medium-high heat. Add the diced onion and sauté for 3-4 minutes until softened and slightly browned.
2. Add the crushed garlic, dried oregano, and calypso chicken dried spice seasoning to the pot and stir to combine. Cook for 1-2 minutes until fragrant.
3. Add all the sliced mushrooms to the pot and stir well. Cook for 10-12 minutes until the mushrooms release their liquid and start to brown.
4. Add the soy sauce/tamari or coconut aminos to the pot and stir to combine. Cook for another 2-3 minutes until the liquid has evaporated and the mushrooms are nicely browned.
5. Add the coconut milk, almond milk, and chicken bone broth to the pot and stir well to combine. Bring the soup to a simmer and cook for 15-20 minutes until the flavors have melded together.
6. Taste the soup and add salt and pepper as needed to season to your liking.
7. Remove the pot from heat and let the soup cool for a few minutes.
8. Using an immersion blender or a regular blender, puree the soup until smooth and creamy.
9. Serve the mushroom soup hot, garnished with fresh herbs or croutons if desired.
10. Enjoy!

This is a great meal to add to any menu any day of the week. Great to have alongside a glass of white wine.

Here are the estimated nutrition facts for one serving (assuming this recipe serves 6):

Calories: 164 Total Fat: 10g Saturated Fat: 6g Trans Fat: 0g Cholesterol: 0mg

Sodium: 595mg Total Carbohydrates: 14g Dietary Fiber: 3g Sugars: 5g Protein: 7g

RAMEN
WITH RICE NOODLES

This is one of my favourite recipes when I am feeling sick or even when I am wanting to make something heart warming.

SERVINGS	TIME	DIFFICULTY	CALORIES
4	30 min	Easy	236 kcal

INGREDIENTS

2.5 cups chicken broth

1 pack miso soup

1 tsp honey

2 tsp soy sauce

1 tbsp sesame oil

3 tbsp. chopped chive

6 oz. flat rice noodles

1 tbsp sesame seeds

3 cups boiling water

DIRECTIONS

1. In a large pot, bring the chicken broth to a simmer over medium heat.
2. Add the miso soup to the pot and stir well until fully dissolved.
3. Add the honey, soy sauce, sesame oil, and chopped chive to the pot and stir well to combine. Let the soup simmer for 5-10 minutes to allow the flavors to meld together.
4. In a separate pot, cook the flat rice noodles according to the package instructions. Drain and rinse the noodles under cold water to stop the cooking process and prevent them from becoming mushy.
5. Add the cooked noodles to the soup and stir gently to combine.
6. Add the boiling water to the soup to adjust the consistency and taste. If the soup is too salty, add more water. If it's not flavorful enough, add more soy sauce or miso soup.
7. Toast the sesame seeds in a dry pan over medium heat for 1-2 minutes until golden brown and fragrant.
8. Ladle the miso noodle soup into bowls and garnish with toasted sesame seeds and additional chopped chive.

NOTES

I love a bowl of noodles when it's movie or episode time. This is one of my favorite meals for one person. Here are the estimated nutrition facts for one serving of this miso noodle soup recipe (assuming this recipe serves 4): Calories: 236
Total Fat: 5g Saturated Fat: 1g Trans Fat: 0g Cholesterol: 2mg Sodium: 1120mg Total Carbohydrates: 39g Dietary Fiber: 2g Sugars: 3g
Protein: 9g

ASIAN BROCCOLI

Stir fry broccoli is one of those amazing, quick meals that you just have to love.

SERVINGS
2-3

TIME
30 min

DIFFICULTY
Easy

CALORIES
323 kcal

INGREDIENTS

1 large head of broccoli, chopped into florets

1 tablespoon ginger, minced

2 cloves garlic, minced

2 tablespoons soy sauce

1 tablespoon sesame oil

1/4 cup water

Salt and pepper to taste

Optional: sesame seeds for garnish

DIRECTIONS

1. Preheat your oven to 400°F (200°C).
2. In a large mixing bowl, toss the broccoli florets with the minced ginger and garlic.
3. In a small mixing bowl, whisk together the soy sauce and sesame oil.
4. Pour the soy sauce and sesame oil mixture over the broccoli, and toss well to combine.
5. Spread the broccoli in a single layer on a baking sheet. Add water to the baking sheet.
6. Season the broccoli with salt and pepper to taste.
7. Bake in the preheated oven for 15-20 minutes or until the broccoli is tender and slightly browned.
8. Optional: Sprinkle sesame seeds over the top of the cooked broccoli before serving.

NOTES

This is one of my favorite go-tos. Calories: 323 (without sesame seeds) or 375 (with sesame seeds) Protein: 14g Carbohydrates: 31g Fiber: 8g Fat: 21g Saturated fat: 3g

SOBA NOODLES
With Mushrooms

SERVINGS
2

TIME
18 min

DIFFICULTY
Easy

CALORIES
357 kcal

INGREDIENTS

1/2 cup soba noodles

1/4 cup chopped broccoli

1/2 cup sliced mushrooms

1/2 block of firm tofu, pressed and cubed

3 tbsp chopped chives

2 tbsp sesame oil

2 tbsp tamari sauce

3 cups chopped bok choy

2 tbsp grated ginger

1 tbsp corn starch

1 tbsp garlic powder

1 tbsp all seasoning

DIRECTIONS

1. Cook soba noodles according to package instructions. Drain and set aside.
2. In a large skillet or wok, heat sesame oil over medium-high heat.
3. Add chopped broccoli and sliced mushrooms, stir-fry for 2-3 minutes.
4. Add cubed tofu to the skillet and stir-fry for 5 minutes, until lightly browned on all sides.
5. Add chopped bok choy and grated ginger, stir-fry for an additional 2-3 minutes.
6. In a small bowl, whisk together tamari sauce, corn starch, garlic powder, and all seasoning. Pour mixture over the vegetables and tofu in the skillet, stirring constantly until sauce thickens.
7. Add cooked soba noodles to the skillet, toss everything together and cook for an additional 1-2 minutes.
8. Remove from heat, sprinkle with chopped chives, and serve hot.

NOTES

Nutrition information (per serving): Calories: 357 kcal Fat: 14.3 g Carbohydrates: 39.7 g Fiber: 5.8 g Sugar: 4.4 g Protein: 17.6 g

SUMMER ROLLS

Summer rolls are a great choice when it comes to wanting a light and delicious meal or sharing snack.

SERVINGS	TIME	DIFFICULTY	CALORIES
2	15 min	Easy	435 kcal

Ingredients

10 spring roll rice paper wrappers

1 large carrot, peeled and julienned

1 large cucumber, julienned (you can peel, but I don't)

1/2 of a large red pepper, julienned

1/3 cup chopped purple cabbage

1 ounce cooked rice vermicelli (optional)

1 avocado

sliced handful fresh cilantro (and/or mint, basil)

5 large green lettuce leaves (romaine, butter, etc), torn in half

20 medium cooked shrimp, peeled and sliced in half length-wise sesame seeds for garnish (optional)

Cabbage noodles/rice

Directions

1. Prep all the ingredients and set them aside.
2. Fill a shallow dish with warm water and dip one rice paper wrapper into the water until it's pliable, about 10-15 seconds.
3. Place the softened rice paper wrapper onto a clean surface, such as a cutting board.
4. Arrange a few pieces of carrot, cucumber, red pepper, and cabbage in the center of the wrapper.
5. Add a small amount of cooked rice vermicelli (if using), avocado slices, a few sprigs of cilantro/mint/basil, and 2 halves of cooked shrimp.
6. Fold the bottom edge of the wrapper up over the filling, then fold in the sides, and roll up tightly.
7. Repeat with the remaining ingredients to make 10 summer rolls.
8. Serve the summer rolls with your favorite dipping sauce and garnish with sesame seeds if desired.
9. Enjoy these refreshing and healthy summer rolls as a light meal or appetizer!

NOTES

This is one of my favorite go-tos when it comes to keeping lean and enjoying healthy bites. Nutrition facts: The exact nutrition information may vary depending on the specific ingredients used and the size of the rolls, but here is a general estimate for one roll without dipping sauce:
Calories: approximately 80 Protein: 4g Fat: 4g Carbohydrates: 9g Fiber: 1g Sugar: 1g Sodium: 65mg

CURRY FISH & SQUASH

This is one of my all time favourite monthly meals.

SERVINGS	TIME	DIFFICULTY	CALORIES
2	15 min	Easy	435 kcal

Ingredients

1 tbsp curry seasoning

1 tsp garlic powder

2 tbsp Bajan Wet season seasoned with 2 pieces of white fish or 8 oz shrimp

1 cup of baked squash

1 tbsp olive oil

Pinch salt

Black pepper

1 cup chicken broth

1 hot pepper (optional)

1/2 cup canned chickpeas (optional)

Instructions

1. Heat a large skillet over medium-high heat.
2. Add the olive oil to the skillet and let it heat up.
3. Add the curry seasoning and garlic powder to the skillet and stir for 30 seconds until fragrant.
4. Add the shrimp or fish to the skillet and stir to coat with the seasoning. Cook for 2-3 minutes until the shrimp or fish is cooked through.
5. Add the cubed baked squash to the skillet and stir to combine.
6. Pour in the chicken broth and bring to a simmer.
7. Add a pinch of salt and black pepper to the skillet and stir well.
8. If desired, add the hot pepper to the skillet for some extra heat.
9. Let the curry simmer for 5-7 minutes until the squash is heated through and the flavors have melded together.
10. Serve the curry and shrimp (or fish) hot with rice or naan bread, if desired.
11. Enjoy!

NOTES

There are a few additions you can make to this recipe to make it more fibrous like adding baked cauliflower, or you can add some chickpeas. These are some of my favorites and I enjoy my curries quite brothy so you can add or reduce broth to your enjoyment and liking.

Total Fat: 22.5g Saturated Fat: 22.5g Cholesterol: Varies depending on the type of fish or shrimp used. Sodium:930mg. Total Carbohydrates: 33g. Dietarty Fiber: 10g Sugars:7g Protein: 27g

Dinners for the
Weeknight

CAULIFLOWER
WITH CUMIN

Baked and air fried cauliflower is one of my favorite foods. Cauliflower is a hot ingredient in health and wellness whether it comes up as cauliflower rice and more trending now, people are grilling cauliflower like steaks.

SERVINGS	TIME	DIFFICULTY	CALORIES
4	20 min	Easy	80 kcal

INGREDIENTS

1 head cauliflower

1 tbsp oil

1 2 tsp cumin

1-2 tsp fresh coriander

1 pinch salt

1 pinch black pepper

Optional (1 tsp chili powder)

1 bell pepper cut into thin strips

DIRECTIONS

1. Preheat your oven to 400°F (200°C).
2. Spread the cauliflower florets and bell pepper strips on a baking sheet in a single layer.
3. Drizzle the oil over the cauliflower and bell pepper and sprinkle with cumin, coriander, salt, and black pepper. Toss everything to coat evenly.
4. If using chili powder, sprinkle it over the cauliflower and bell pepper as well.
5. Roast in the preheated oven for 20-25 minutes, or until the cauliflower is tender and lightly browned.
6. Sprinkle with additional fresh coriander before serving, if desired.

NOTES

If you have an air frier these are great in there also. Here are the approximate nutrition facts for the roasted cauliflower with cumin, coriander, and bell peppers recipe: Serving size: 1/4 of the recipe Calories: 80 Total fat: 4.5g Saturated fat: 0.5g Trans fat: 0g Cholesterol: 0mg Sodium: 170mg Total Carbohydrate: 9g Dietary Fiber: 4g Total Sugars: 4g Protein: 3g

STUFFED PEPPERS

When it comes to having a meal in a pepper, this is fun because it adds a boost of colors and flavors in the dish. It is quick and easy to put together after a long day of work or even to have as a side if you are having friends over for a bbq/lunch.

SERVINGS	TIME	DIFFICULTY	CALORIES
2	30 min	Easy	298 kcal

INGREDIENTS

4 bell peppers

1 lb minced chicken

1 onion, diced

1 cup sliced mushrooms

2 tbsp tomato paste

1 cup chicken broth

1 tsp all-purpose seasoning

1/2 tsp black pepper

1 tbsp olive oil

DIRECTIONS

1. Preheat the oven to 375°F (190°C).
2. Cut off the tops of the bell peppers and remove the seeds and membranes from inside. Rinse the peppers and set them aside.
3. In a skillet, heat the olive oil over medium heat. Add the diced onion and cook until softened, about 5 minutes.
4. Add the sliced mushrooms to the skillet and cook for another 5 minutes.
5. Add the minced chicken to the skillet and cook until browned, breaking up any clumps with a wooden spoon.
6. Stir in the tomato paste, chicken broth, all-purpose seasoning, and black pepper. Let simmer for 5 minutes.
7. Spoon the chicken mixture into each of the bell peppers until they are filled to the top.
8. Place the stuffed peppers in a baking dish and pour the remaining chicken broth over the top.
9. Cover the baking dish with foil and bake for 30-35 minutes, or until the peppers are tender and the chicken is cooked through.
10. Remove the foil from the baking dish and bake for an additional 10-15 minutes, or until the tops of the peppers are lightly browned.
11. Remove from the oven and let cool for a few minutes before serving.

NOTES

Here are the approximate nutrition facts per serving for this stuffed bell peppers recipe (assuming 4 servings in total): Calories: 298 Fat: 15g Saturated Fat: 3g Trans Fat: 0g Cholesterol: 98mg Sodium: 402mg Carbohydrates: 13g Fiber: 4g Sugar: 7g Protein: 25g

Note: These nutrition facts are approximate and may vary based on the specific ingredients and cooking methods used.

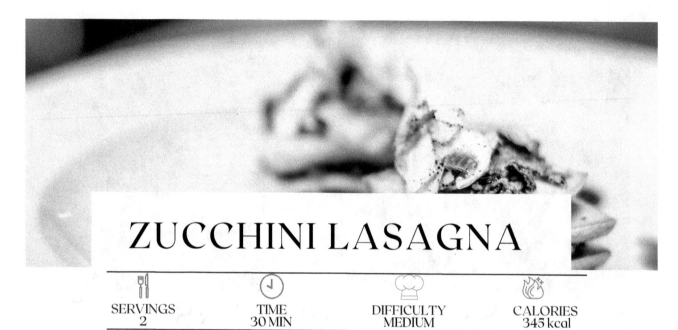

ZUCCHINI LASAGNA

SERVINGS	TIME	DIFFICULTY	CALORIES
2	30 MIN	MEDIUM	345 kcal

INGREDIENTS

1 pack minced chicken

3 small or 1-2 large zucchini

(enough for about 25 slices)

1 onion, chopped

5 diced tomatoes

3 celery stalks, chopped

1/4 cup tomato paste

1/2 tsp garlic powder

1/4 cup fresh basil, chopped

2 tbsp fresh oregano, chopped

1 tbsp fresh or dried thyme

1/2 cup goat cheese

1 egg

1/2 cup stock (chicken or

vegetable)

2 tsp paprika

Pinch of cayenne pepper

2 tbsp fresh rosemary, chopped

1 1/2 cups vegan grated

mozzarella

DIRECTIONS

1. Preheat the oven to 375°F.
2. In a large skillet, cook the minced chicken over medium heat until browned. Drain any excess fat.
3. Add the chopped onion, diced tomatoes, chopped celery, tomato paste, garlic powder, paprika, cayenne pepper, and fresh herbs to the skillet. Stir to combine and cook for 5-7 minutes, until the vegetables are tender.
4. In a separate bowl, whisk together the goat cheese and egg until well combined.
5. Grease a 9x13 inch baking dish with cooking spray.
6. Lay the zucchini slices in a single layer on the bottom of the baking dish, covering the entire surface.
7. Spread half of the chicken and vegetable mixture on top of the zucchini.
8. Spoon half of the goat cheese mixture on top of the chicken and vegetable mixture.
9. Repeat the layers, ending with a layer of zucchini on top.
10. Pour the stock over the top layer of zucchini, making sure it is evenly distributed.
11. Sprinkle the vegan grated mozzarella on top of the lasagna.
12. Cover the baking dish with foil and bake in the preheated oven for 30 minutes.
13. Remove the foil and continue baking for an additional 15-20 minutes, until the cheese is melted and bubbly.
14. Let the lasagna cool for a few minutes before serving.

Here are the estimated nutrition facts and calorie information for this grain-free lasagna recipe, based on the ingredients and measurements listed:
Servings: 8 Calories per serving: approximately 290 Macronutrients: Protein: 23g Fat: 15g Carbohydrates: 15g Fiber: 3g
Sugar: 8g

QUINOA TABOULEH

This is one of my favourite meals that is so refreshing and hydrating with the pasley and cold temperatures.

SERVINGS
2

TIME
30 MIN

DIFFICULTY
MEDIUM

CALORIES
345 kcal

INGREDIENTS

1 cup cooked quinoa

2 cups chopped tomatoes, about 2 large

11/2 cups chopped cucumbers

1/2 cup chopped onion (can substitute green onions)

1 cups fresh parsley, finely chopped

Dressing:

3 Tablespoons olive oil

3 Lemons squeezed

2 garlic clove, grated

1/2 teaspoon ground cumin

1/2 teaspoon salt

1/4 teaspoon black pepper

DIRECTIONS

1. In a large bowl, combine the cooked quinoa, chopped tomatoes, cucumbers, chopped onion, and fresh parsley.
2. In a small bowl, whisk together the olive oil, lemon juice, grated garlic, ground cumin, salt, and black pepper until well combined.
3. Pour the dressing over the quinoa and vegetables and toss well to combine.
4. Taste and adjust seasoning as needed, adding more salt or pepper to taste.
5. Chill the salad in the refrigerator for at least 30 minutes to allow the flavors to meld together.
6. Serve the salad chilled and enjoy!

Notes

Quinoa is a great ingredient to have in fresh salads. I am a big fan and it is filling and popular to make salads. This salad is a great side dish for grilled meats or fish, or can be served as a light and refreshing lunch on its own. It's also vegan and gluten-free, making it a healthy and versatile option for any occasion. Here are the estimated nutrition facts for this recipe, based on the specific quantities and ingredients listed: Calories: 345 Protein: 9g Carbohydrates: 43g Fiber: 10g Fat: 17g Saturated Fat: 2g Sodium: 399mg Potassium: 1014mg Vitamin A: 2713IU Vitamin C: 104mg Calcium: 108mg Iron: 4mg

FRITTERS

Zucchini fritters are some of my favorite foods ever. Air fryers are in almost every home now and are a great way to keep lean and ensure that you enjoy your dietary choices in addition to keep your calories down.

SERVINGS	TIME	DIFFICULTY	CALORIES
2	30 min	HARD	399 kcal

INGREDIENTS

1 cup shredded zucchini

2 medium eggs

1 onion, shredded

1/2 tsp garlic powder

1 tbsp coconut oil

1/4 cup almond flour

1 tbsp fresh parsley, chopped

DIRECTIONS

1. In a large bowl, whisk together the eggs and garlic powder until well combined.
2. Add the shredded zucchini, shredded onion, almond flour, and chopped parsley to the bowl and stir well to combine.
3. Heat the coconut oil in a large skillet over medium-high heat. Use air frier to cut calories and reduce fat.
4. Once the oil is hot, drop spoonfuls of the zucchini mixture into the skillet, flattening each one with the back of a spoon.
5. Cook the fritters for 2-3 minutes on each side, or until golden brown and crispy.
6. Once the fritters are cooked, transfer them to a plate lined with paper towels to absorb any excess oil.
7. Serve the fritters warm and enjoy!

NOTES

You can swap out coconut oil for olive oil and use the air frier to ensure that you get the best result when it comes to crisp and delicious choices. Here are the estimated nutrition facts for this recipe, based on the specific quantities and ingredients listed: Calories: 399 Protein: 14g Carbohydrates: 13g. Fiber: 4g Fat: 33g Saturated Fat: 12g Sodium: 180mg Potassium: 417mg Vitamin A: 743IU Vitamin C: 17mg Calcium: 91mg Iron: 2mg Note that these values are estimates and may vary depending on the specific ingredients and brands used. Also, keep in mind that the serving size may affect the nutritional content per serving.

POPCORN CHICKEN GF

Chicken bites are always a favourite choice to have on any menu.

SERVINGS
2-4

TIME
20 min

DIFFICULTY
MEDIUM

CALORIES
360 kcal

INGREDIENTS

1-2 chicken breast cut into strips seasoned with Mrs. Dash Italian herb or Chef Paul seasoning mix or Caribbean seasoning mix

2 tsp paprika

1 pinch cayenne pepper

1 tsp black pepper

1 cup gluten free flour (Bob's Red Mill)

2 tbsp garlic powder

1 clove garlic

2 sprigs rosemary

1 tsp salt

1 egg

DIRECTIONS

1. In a shallow bowl, whisk together the gluten-free flour, garlic powder, salt, paprika, cayenne pepper, and black pepper.
2. In another shallow bowl, whisk together the egg, minced garlic, and chopped rosemary.
3. Dip each chicken strip into the egg mixture, making sure it is well coated.
4. Next, coat each chicken strip in the seasoned flour mixture, shaking off any excess.
5. Preheat your air fryer to 375°F.
6. Spray the basket of your air fryer with cooking spray.
7. Place the chicken strips in a single layer in the basket of the air fryer.
8. Spray the chicken strips lightly with cooking spray.
9. Air fry the chicken for 10-12 minutes, or until golden brown and cooked through.
10. Once the chicken is cooked through, remove it from the air fryer and place it on a plate lined with paper towels to absorb any excess oil.
11. Serve the popcorn chicken hot and enjoy!

NOTES

This recipe is perfect for a quick and easy dinner or as a fun snack. The gluten-free flour and seasoning mix options make it customizable for different dietary needs and preferences. Here are the estimated nutrition facts for this air fryer popcorn chicken recipe: Calories: 360 Protein: 43g Carbohydrates: 29g Fiber: 2g Fat: 8g Saturated Fat: 2g Cholesterol: 220mg Sodium: 1093mg Potassium: 570mg Vitamin A: 596IU Vitamin C: 2mg Calcium: 34mg Iron: 3mg Note that these values are estimates and may vary depending on the specific ingredients and brands used. The nutritional information may also vary depending on the size of the chicken strips and how much flour and egg mixture is used for coating.

FRIED FISH

When the grill is on we are big fans of putting the veggies on because it is a great side choice and tastes really good.

SERVINGS
4

TIME
80 min

DIFFICULTY
MEDIUM

CALORIES
440 kcal

INGREDIENTS

4 lbs. boneless or flying fish

2 tbsp. wet seasoning (of your choice)

1 cup cassava flour

1/4 cup coconut flour

1 tsp paprika

1/4 tsp salt

Cracked pepper (optional)

1 tsp garlic powder

1 tsp onion powder

Caribbean chicken seasoning (to taste)

1/4 cup oil for frying

DIRECTIONS

1. Preheat the air fryer to 400°F (200°C).
2. Rinse the fish and pat it dry with paper towels.
3. In a bowl, mix together the wet seasoning and set it aside.
4. In a separate bowl, mix together the cassava flour, coconut flour, paprika, salt, cracked pepper, garlic powder, onion powder, and Caribbean chicken seasoning.
5. Dip each piece of fish into the wet seasoning, then into the flour mixture, making sure to coat it well on all sides.
6. Place the fish in the air fryer basket, making sure not to overcrowd it.
7. Drizzle the oil over the fish.
8. Air fry the fish for 10-12 minutes, or until it is crispy and cooked through.
9. Serve hot with your favorite dipping sauce.

NOTES

The calorie and nutrition facts will vary depending on the type of fish used, the exact amount of ingredients used, and the number of servings. However, in general, air frying fish can be a healthier cooking option as it uses less oil and retains more nutrients compared to deep-frying. Assuming that the recipe yields 6 servings and that mahi mahi is used, here are the estimated calorie and nutrition facts: Calories per serving: 430 Total Fat: 19g Saturated Fat: 5g Cholesterol: 212mg Sodium: 286mg Total Carbohydrates: 13g Dietary Fiber: 3g Total Sugars: 0g Protein: 52g

BARRACUDA CEVICHE

Fresh fish is such a fun choice to whip up with friends. This is one of my favorite foods and there are a variety of fish that you can use to make this fun and flavorful sharing dish.

SERVINGS	TIME	DIFFICULTY	CALORIES
4	80 min	MEDIUM	140 kcal

INGREDIENTS

1 pound fresh barracuda fillets, skin removed and cut into small cubes

3/4 cup freshly squeezed lime juice

1/2 cup freshly squeezed lemon juice

1/4 cup freshly squeezed orange juice

1 jalapeño pepper, seeds removed and finely diced

1 tomato, diced

1/2 cup cucumber diced

1/2 cup chopped cilantro

1/4 cup chopped shadow beni

Salt and pepper, to taste

Plantain chips or lettuce leaves, for serving

NOTES

DIRECTIONS

1. Place the barracuda cubes in a glass or ceramic bowl. Pour the lime and lemon juice over the fish, making sure it is fully submerged. Let it marinate in the refrigerator for about 30 minutes to 1 hour. The citrus juices will "cook" the fish and give it a tender texture.
2. Meanwhile, prepare the cucumber, jalapeño pepper, tomato, cilantro, and mint. Finely dice the jalapeño pepper, and dice the tomato. Chop the cilantro and herbs. Set aside.
3. After the fish has marinated, drain off most of the citrus juice. Leave just enough to keep the ceviche moist. The fish should be opaque and have a slightly firm texture.
4. Add the diced jalapeño pepper, tomato, cilantro, herbs and mint to the bowl with the fish. Gently toss everything together until well combined. Season with salt and pepper to taste.
5. Let the ceviche sit in the refrigerator for another 15-30 minutes to allow the flavors to meld together.
6. Serve the barracuda ceviche chilled with tortilla chips or lettuce leaves for scooping. Enjoy the refreshing and zesty flavors!
7. Note: Ceviche is best consumed within a few hours of preparation for optimal freshness and flavor. If you prefer a spicier ceviche, you can leave the seeds in the jalapeño pepper or add a few dashes of hot sauce to the mixture.
8. Bon appétit!

The calorie and nutrition facts will vary depending on the type of fish used, the exact amount of ingredients used, and the number of servings. However, in general, air frying fish can be a healthier cooking option as it uses less oil and retains more nutrients compared to deep-frying. Assuming that the recipe yields 6 servings and that mahi mahi is used, here are the estimated calorie and nutrition facts: Calories per 4 serving: 430 Total Fat: 19g Saturated Fat: 5g Cholesterol: 212mg Sodium: 286mg Total Carbohydrates: 13g Dietary Fiber: 3g Total Sugars: 0g Protein: 52g

75

CAJUN WHOLE CHICKEN

The healthier alternative to deep fried chicken.
Quick, easy, tasty. This is great for meal prep and a weekend menu choice.

SERVINGS	TIME	DIFFICULTY	CALORIES
4	80 min	MEDIUM	140 kcal

INGREDIENTS

1 Whole chicken

¼ pack of Bajan wet seasoning

1 tsp cajun powder

1tsp dried paprika and cayenne pepper dried spice mix.

¼ tsp salt

¼ tsp black pepper

1 tbsp. olive oil

1 orange

DIRECTIONS

1. Preheat the oven to 375°F (190°C).

2. Rinse the chicken inside and out with cold water, and pat it dry with paper towels.

3. In a small bowl, mix together the Bajan seasoning, dried spices, salt, and black pepper.

4. Rub the spice mixture all over the chicken, making sure to get some under the skin and in the cavity. Add an orange inside of the chicken.

5. Place the chicken in a roasting pan or baking dish, breast side up. You can flip 3/4 time and flip back for the final 10 minutes.

6. Drizzle the olive oil over the chicken, and use your hands to rub it all over the skin.

7. Roast the chicken in the preheated oven for about 1 hour and 20 minutes, or until the internal temperature reaches 165°F (75°C). You can broil for the last 10 minutes.

8. Remove the chicken from the oven and let it rest for 10-15 minutes before carving and serving.

NOTES

Servings: 4
Calories: Approximately 137 kcal (based on the chicken and olive oil) Total Fat: Approximately 7.7 grams (based on the chicken and olive oil)
Saturated Fat: Approximately 1.9 grams (based on the chicken and olive oil) Carbohydrates: Approximately 1.5 grams (based on the seasoning and orange) Fiber: Approximately 0.75 grams (based on the orange) Protein: Approximately 15 grams (based on the chicken)

VEGAN BURGER WRAP

My Favourite Way To Keep Lean Is With a Vegan Burger Wrap When I get Burger Cravings.

SERVINGS	TIME	DIFFICULTY	CALORIES
2	15 min	Medium	263 kcal

INGREDIENTS

1.5 cup cooked black beans, drained and rinsed

3/4 cup chopped mushrooms

2 onions, chopped

3 garlic cloves, minced

1/4 teaspoon salt

1/4 teaspoon Ms. Dash seasoning blend

2 sprigs thyme, leaves stripped and chopped

1/8 teaspoon cayenne pepper

1/4 teaspoon paprika

1 Tomato

6 tablespoons water

6 tablespoons Bob's Red Mill all-purpose flour

3 tablespoons olive oil

2 teaspoons paprika

DIRECTIONS

1. In a food processor, pulse the black beans, mushrooms, onions, garlic, salt, Ms. Dash, thyme, cayenne, paprika, and celery leaves until well combined. Transfer the mixture to a bowl.

2. Add the water and flour to the bowl and mix well until a thick, dough-like consistency is formed.

3. Divide the mixture into 4 equal portions and shape into patties.

4. Heat the olive oil in a non-stick skillet over medium heat. Add the patties and cook for 4-5 minutes on each side, until golden brown and crispy. For a quick alternative, you can purchase a ready made burger and serve it up the same way or take to a bbq.

5. Serve the burgers on buns with your favorite toppings and condiments. Note: You can also grill or bake the burgers instead of pan-frying if you prefer.

6. Serve on a large grilled Portobello mushroom with lettuce, tomato & some hummus or place in a wrap for a quick meal with your favorite condiments.

7. Store remainders in the freezer for quick warming up during the week.

NOTES

Nutrition facts per serving (1 burger patty): Calories: 263 Fat: 11g Saturated Fat: 1g Sodium: 183mg Carbohydrates: 32g Fiber: 10g Sugar: 3g Protein: 10g

TUNA PLANTAIN TACO

Fresh Tuna is always a favourite of mine

SERVINGS
2

TIME
15 min

DIFFICULTY
Easy

CALORIES
364 kcal

INGREDIENTS

12 oz fresh ahi tuna

2 tablespoons sesame oil

2 tablespoons soy sauce

1 cup coleslaw mix

1/4 cup chopped cilantro

2 green onions, chopped

1 lime, cut into wedges

8 small corn tortillas

or 8 servings of Plantain Tostones Chips

NOTES

DIRECTIONS

1. Preheat a grill or grill pan to medium-high heat.
2. Cut the ahi tuna into small bite-sized pieces.
3. In a medium-sized bowl, whisk together the sesame oil and soy sauce.
4. Add the tuna to the bowl and toss to coat with the marinade.
5. Grill the tuna for 1-2 minutes on each side, until lightly charred but still pink in the center.
6. While the tuna is grilling, prepare the coleslaw. In a separate bowl, mix together the coleslaw mix, chopped cilantro, and chopped green onions.
7. Warm the corn tortillas on the grill for 30 seconds on each side.
8. To assemble the tacos, place a spoonful of coleslaw on each tortilla, followed by a few pieces of grilled tuna. Squeeze a lime wedge over the top.
9. Serve and enjoy!

Calories: 364 Total Fat: 13.2g Saturated Fat: 2.3g Cholesterol: 60mg Sodium: 1050mg Total Carbohydrates: 24.9g Dietary Fiber: 4.1g Total Sugars: 4.7g Protein: 37.6g
Note: These values may vary depending on the specific brands and quantities of ingredients used in the recipe.

SKEWERS

Skewers are a great choice to have for any social occasion and wonderful choice for you to get some extra flavors in your life. The vegetarian version for these are fun to have when you have guests alongside the chicken skewers. Include a mix.

SERVINGS	TIME	DIFFICULTY	CALORIES
4	30 min	Easy	90 kcal

INGREDIENTS

2 large chicken breasts, cut into 1-inch cubes

1 chive stalk, finely chopped

1 tsp sea salt

2 tbsp. olive oil

1 tbsp. coconut oil

2 tbsp. paprika

1 tsp. cinnamon

1/4 tsp. cayenne pepper

DIRECTIONS

1. In a large bowl, mix together the chicken cubes, chive, sea salt, olive oil, and coconut oil until the chicken is well coated.
2. Add the paprika, cinnamon, and cayenne pepper to the bowl and toss until the chicken is evenly coated.
3. Thread the chicken onto skewers, leaving a little space between each cube.
4. Heat a grill or grill pan to medium-high heat. Grill the skewers, turning occasionally, until the chicken is cooked through and slightly charred, about 8-10 minutes.
5. Remove the skewers from the grill and sprinkle with additional sea salt, if desired.
6. Enjoy your perfect skewers!

NOTES

Skewers are amazing when having friends over or even for a family fun quick meal. I love serving chicken skewers with fresh hummus and Arabic style salads. Calories: 90 Total Fat: 5.8g Saturated Fat: 1.8g Trans Fat: 0g Cholesterol: 24mg Sodium: 183.5mg Total Carbohydrates: 1.5g Dietary Fiber: 0.75g Sugars: 0.25g. Protein: 8.25g

Snacks and Dips

Sharing or Solo

HUMMUS WITH SPICES

Hummus is one of my go-to recipes and it is on my menu on a monthly basis because it is so flavorful and packed with heart-healthy fibre.

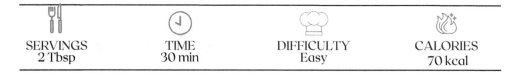

| SERVINGS 2 Tbsp | TIME 30 min | DIFFICULTY Easy | CALORIES 70 kcal |

INGREDIENTS

1 can (15 ounces) chickpeas or white beans, drained and rinsed

1/4 cup reserved chickpea liquid

1 medium garlic clove, chopped

1/2 cup tahini

1/4 cup fresh lemon juice, more to taste

1 teaspoon fine sea salt

1/4 cup extra-virgin olive oil

2 tablespoons chopped fresh parsley

1/4 teaspoon toasted whole cumin seeds, ground

1/4 teaspoon toasted whole coriander seeds, ground

Pinch of paprika, for garnish

DIRECTIONS

1. In a food processor or blender, add the chickpeas, reserved liquid, and chopped garlic. Process until the mixture is smooth and creamy.
2. Add the tahini, lemon juice, and salt to the food processor and process until everything is well combined.
3. With the food processor running, slowly pour in the olive oil and process until the hummus is smooth and creamy.
4. Add the chopped parsley, ground cumin, and ground coriander to the food processor and pulse a few times to combine.
5. Taste the hummus and adjust the seasoning with additional lemon juice, salt, or olive oil, if needed.
6. Transfer the hummus to a serving bowl and sprinkle with a pinch of paprika for garnish.
7. Serve the hummus with pita bread, vegetables, or crackers.
8. Enjoy your delicious homemade hummus!

NOTES

Hummus is my favorite dip to have in the fridge or take to the beach or when I have friends over by the pool. I love to include it in my wraps, or dip in some cucumber sticks or plantain chips. Calories: 70 Total Fat: 5g Saturated Fat: 1g Trans Fat: 0g Cholesterol: 0mg Sodium: 150mg Total Carbohydrates: 4g Dietary Fiber: 1g Sugars: 0g Protein: 2g

CHEESY POPCORN VEGAN

Cheesy organic popcorn is certainly one of my all-time favorite snacks when having friends over or even watching a movie.

SERVINGS	TIME	DIFFICULTY	CALORIES
4	10 min	Easy	55 kcal

INGREDIENTS

Makes 4 servings
(about 10 cups)

Ingredients

½ cup organic
popcorn seeds

2 tbsp. nutritional
yeast

1 tsp pink salt

1 tsp garlic powder
(optional)

2-3 tbsp. olive oil

DIRECTIONS

1. Preheat a large pot over medium-high heat.
2. Add the olive oil to the pot and swirl it around to coat the bottom.
3. Add the popcorn seeds to the pot and cover with a tight-fitting lid.
4. Shake the pot occasionally to prevent the popcorn from burning and to ensure even popping.
5. Once the popping has slowed down, remove the pot from the heat and let it sit for a few seconds to allow any remaining kernels to pop.
6. In a separate bowl, mix together the nutritional yeast, pink salt, and garlic powder (if using).
7. Pour the popcorn into a large bowl and sprinkle the seasoning mixture over the top.
8. Toss the popcorn to evenly coat with the seasoning.
9. Enjoy your homemade popcorn as a delicious snack!

NOTES

Nothing like a good bowl of popcorn with friends, family, and even a rainy movie day. Serving size: 1 cup popped popcorn

Calories: 55 Total fat: 3.8g Saturated fat: 0.5g Cholesterol: 0mg Sodium: 200mg Total carbohydrates: 4.2g

Dietary fiber: 0.7g Sugars: 0.1g Protein: 1.3g

Note: Nutrition facts may vary depending on the brand and type of ingredients used.

GUACAMOLE

YUMMINESS

Guacamole is one of my favorite dips to enjoy. Summer is when this fruit is most abundant.
It amazes me how large the Caribbean Avocados are.

SERVINGS	TIME	DIFFICULTY	CALORIES
2	15 min	Easy	322 kcal

INGREDIENTS

1 Caribbean avocado or 2 Haas avocados, peeled and pitted

2 tsp chopped cilantro/ shadow beni

Juice of 2 limes

Black pepper, to taste

Sea salt, to taste

Optional: chili flakes, to taste

DIRECTIONS

1. Mash the avocado in a bowl using a fork or a potato masher.
2. Add the chopped cilantro/shadow beni and lime juice to the mashed avocado and mix well.
3. Season the dip with black pepper and sea salt, to taste.
4. Add chili flakes, if desired, for some extra heat.
5. Serve the avocado dip with tortilla chips or as a topping for tacos, sandwiches, or salads.

NOTES

Guacamole is such a favorite when it comes to beach dips, friends coming over dips, and Mexican family nights. You can't go wrong with this recipe. Here is the estimated nutrition information for a medium-sized Caribbean avocado:
Calories: 322 Fat: 29g Carbohydrates: 17g Fiber: 13g Protein: 4g Sodium: 6mg
Adding the other ingredients will not significantly change the nutrition information.

BULJOL
TACOS

This recipe is for buljol which is a codfish dip made with dried cod similar to a salsa with the seasonings. It is very popular but you can also make them into tacos for a fun mini meal.

🍴 SERVINGS	🕐 TIME	👨‍🍳 DIFFICULTY	🔥 CALORIES
8	30 min	Easy	515 kcal

INGREDIENTS

1 pack salted codfish

2 tomatoes diced

1 cucumber diced

1 bell pepper diced

2 limes

1 onion diced

4 tbsp. olive oil

½ tsp black pepper

Wraps or Taco Shells

DIRECTIONS

1. Drain and rinse the soaked saltfish, then boil it in a pot of water for about 10 minutes until cooked.
2. Let the saltfish cool, then use your hands to shred it into small pieces.
3. In a large bowl, combine the shredded saltfish, diced tomatoes, cucumber, and bell pepper.
4. In a small bowl, whisk together the lime juice, olive oil, and black pepper.
5. Pour the dressing over the saltfish and vegetables, and toss to combine.
6. Serve the saltfish salad chilled or at room temperature.
7. Note: You can adjust the amount of olive oil and black pepper to your taste preferences. This recipe serves 4 as a side dish.

NOTES

Calories: 515 per whole dish.
Total Fat: 41g Saturated Fat: 5.9g Polyunsaturated Fat: 5.2g Monounsaturated Fat: 28g Cholesterol: 60mg Sodium: 1119mg Potassium: 939mg Total Carbohydrates: 16g Dietary Fiber: 4g Sugars: 6g Protein: 24g Vitamin A: 22% Vitamin C: 95% Calcium: 9% Iron: 21% Note: Nutritional values may vary depending on the specific type/brand of salt fish used.

TOMATO SALSA

SPICY

Salsas are so refreshing and hit the spot when you feel like you would like a tangy snack dip or even topping for a meal.

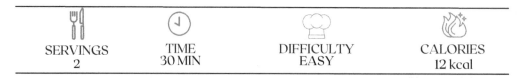

SERVINGS 2	TIME 30 MIN	DIFFICULTY EASY	CALORIES 12 kcal

INGREDIENTS

4 tomatoes, diced

1 small onion, diced

2 limes, juiced

1 garlic clove, finely chopped

2 tbsp chopped cilantro or shadow beni

1 chili pepper, finely chopped

DIRECTIONS

1. In a medium-sized bowl, combine the diced tomatoes and onion.
2. Add the juice of 2 limes to the bowl.
3. Add the finely chopped garlic and chili pepper to the bowl.
4. Add the chopped cilantro or shadow beni to the bowl and mix well.
5. Serve immediately or chill in the refrigerator until ready to serve.

NOTES

When it comes to salsa and chips, this is by far one of my ultimate favorite foods on the planet. I love to have it with plantain chips personally. Nutrition facts: Serving size: 1/4 cup Calories: 12 Total fat: 0.2g Saturated fat: 0g Cholesterol: 0mg Sodium: 1mg Total carbohydrates: 3g Dietary fiber: 1g Sugars: 1g Protein: 0.5g

Note: Nutrition facts may vary slightly depending on the size and ripeness of the tomatoes and the type of chili pepper used.

GREEN PEA PESTO

GREEN PEA PESTO DIP

SERVINGS	TIME	DIFFICULTY	CALORIES
1/4 Cup	30 min	Easy	120-150 kcal

INGREDIENTS

1 1/2 cups frozen green peas, thawed

1/4 cup fresh basil leaves

1/4 cup grated vegan Parmesan for a dairy-free version)

1/4 cup pine nuts or walnuts

1 clove garlic, minced

2 tablespoons lemon juice

1/4 cup extra virgin olive oil

Salt and pepper, to taste

DIRECTIONS

1. In a food processor, combine the green peas, basil leaves, mint leaves, Parmesan cheese, pine nuts or walnuts, minced garlic, and lemon juice.
2. Pulse until the ingredients start to come together.
3. While the processor is running, slowly drizzle in the olive oil until the pesto reaches a smooth and creamy consistency.
4. Season with salt and pepper to taste.
5. Transfer the Green Pea Pesto Dip to a serving bowl.
6. Place it on the serving platter alongside the other dips and veggie sticks.

NOTES

This dip is wonderful. I love to have it with plantain chips personally. Nutrition facts: Serving size: 1/4 cup Calories: 12 Total fat: 0.2g
Saturated fat: 0g Cholesterol: 0mg Sodium: 1mg Total carbohydrates: 3g Dietary fiber: 1g Sugars: 1g Protein: 0.5g
Note: Nutrition facts may vary slightly depending on the size and ripeness of the tomatoes and the type of chili pepper used.

VEGGIE SNACKS

Dips are my favorite when socializing. I am a big fan.

SERVINGS	TIME	DIFFICULTY	CALORIES
5	30 min	Easy	350-400 kcal

INGREDIENTS

1/2 Cup Hummus

1/2 Cup Babaganoush

1/2 Cup Green Pea Dip

1/2 Cup Vegan Chicken Buffalo Dip

2 Cups Veggie Sticks

1 Pack Rice Crackers

1 Pack Plantain Chips

NOTES

DIRECTIONS

Bring out your hummus, babaganoush, green pea dip, vegan chicken buffalo & veggie sticks on a platter to serve with friends.

Beetroot Hummus:
1 serving (approximately 1/4 cup): Around 90-110 calories

Baba Ghanoush:
1 serving (approximately 1/4 cup): Around 60-80 calories

Vegan Buffalo "Chicken" Dip:
1 serving (approximately 1/4 cup): Around 70-90 calories

As for the veggie sticks, the calorie content will depend on the specific vegetables you choose and the portion sizes. Generally, vegetables like carrots, celery, bell peppers, and cucumbers have a low calorie count. You can estimate around 25-50 calories per serving of veggie sticks, depending on the amount consumed.

This is the best to have for weekends either for you and your family or for friends coming over to catch up. Great for a beach day or even as a meal prep day of some home cleaning.

SEXY COCKTAILS

BEVERAGES

SURPRISE YOUR GUESTS

To be enjoyed with a dinner party, meal. Please drink responsibly or try these fun mixes without any alcohols for some mocktail sober experience.

TEQUILA COSMO

2 oz Premium Tequila
1 oz Triple Sec
1 oz Pineapple Juice
1 oz Lime Juice
Pineapple wedge, for garnish

1. Fill a cocktail shaker with ice.
2. Add 2 oz of Tequila to the shaker.
3. Add 1 oz of Triple Sec to the shaker.
4. Add 1 oz of Pineapple Juice to the shaker.
5. Add 1 oz of Lime Juice to the shaker.
6. Shake the ingredients vigorously until well chilled.
7. Strain the mixture into a chilled cocktail glass.
8. Garnish the cocktail with a wedge of pineapple.

Calories: Around 273-340 kcal
Carbohydrates: Around 23-28 grams
Fat: 0 grams
Protein: 0 grams

Martini

Calories: Around 84 calories (calculated using 2.5 oz gin/vodka + 0.5 oz vermouth + 0.5 oz cucumber juice)
Carbohydrates: Approximately 2.2 grams of carbohydrates

2 1/2 OUNCES GIN OR VODKA
1/2 OUNCE DRY VERMOUTH
1/2 OUNCE CUCUMBER JUICE (OPTIONAL)
MIST OF A LEMON PEEL

GARNISH: 2 TO 4 OLIVES OR CUCUMBER SLICE

1. Chill the Martini Glass: Place the martini glass in the freezer for a few minutes to chill it. A chilled glass helps keep the cocktail cool while you enjoy it.
2. Prepare the Cucumber Juice: To make cucumber juice, you can either blend fresh cucumber slices and strain the juice or use a juicer to extract the juice. Make sure the cucumber juice is fresh and free from any added sugars or additives.
3. Combine the Ingredients: In a mixing glass or shaker, add 2 1/2 ounces of gin or vodka, 1/2 ounce of dry vermouth, and 1/2 ounce of cucumber juice.
4. Stir or Shake: You have two options for mixing the cocktail: stirring or shaking. If you prefer a smoother and milder drink, gently stir the ingredients with a bar spoon for about 15-20 seconds. If you like a colder and more diluted cocktail, use a shaker filled with ice and shake the mixture vigorously for about 10-15 seconds.
5. Strain into the Chilled Glass: Carefully strain the mixed cocktail into the chilled martini glass. Using a cocktail strainer or the shaker's built-in strainer will help ensure no ice or pulp enters the glass.
6. Garnish: Take a lemon peel and squeeze it over the cocktail to release its aromatic oils. Then, rub the lemon peel around the rim of the glass before spraying lemon mist on the surface of the drink as a garnish.
7. Serve and Enjoy: Your Cucumber Martini is now ready to be served. Sip and enjoy the refreshing flavors of cucumber and the classic martini base!

Remember to drink responsibly and in moderation. Cheers!

ESPRESSO MARTINI

These are my favourite weekend treat. I am so grateful to be able to have this sugar free alternative at hand to enjoy cocktails with lower amounts of sugar and calories.

Ingredients :

1 shot of espresso

1 1/2 oz vodka

1/2 oz sugar-free coffee liqueur

(e.g. Jordan's Skinny Syrups,

Torani, or similar brand)

1/2 oz sugar-free simple syrup

(e.g. Lakanto or similar brand)

Ice

3 coffee beans for garnish

Notes :

Calorie Count and Nutrition Facts:
1 shot of espresso: 1 calorie, 0g fat, 0g carbs, 0g protein
1 1/2 oz vodka: 97 calories, 0g fat, 0g carbs, 0g protein
1/2 oz sugar-free coffee liqueur: 0 calories, 0g fat, 0g carbs, 0g protein
1/2 oz sugar-free simple syrup: 0 calories, 0g fat, 0g carbs, 0g protein
Total calorie count: 98 calories

Procedure :

1. Brew a shot of espresso and allow it to cool.

2. In a cocktail shaker, combine the cooled espresso, vodka, sugar-free coffee liqueur, and sugar-free simple syrup.

3. Fill the shaker with ice and shake vigorously for 10-15 seconds.

4. Strain the cocktail into a chilled martini glass.

5. Garnish with three coffee beans.

BANANA DAIQUIRI

This beverage screams vacation brunch mode. Add some tequila or vodka with your frozen bananas. Now the recipe lists rum because the Caribbean is famous for the rum. I am not a rum drinker so I am noting my substitutions in this note but for all of you rum drinkers, you will love this one. Get extra exciting to make it a meal with collagen protein powder. Filling, and relaxing. No fuss vacay mode.

Ingredients :

Ingredients:

1.5 cups frozen banana chunks

2 oz premium rum

1/4 cup coconut water

Dash of ground cinnamon

1/2 cup ice

Procedure :

1. Add the frozen banana chunks, rum, ground cinnamon, and ice to a blender.
2. Blend on high until the mixture is smooth and creamy.
3. If the mixture is too thick, add a small amount of water or coconut water to thin it out to your desired consistency.
4. Pour the daiquiri into a chilled glass.
5. Garnish with a slice of fresh banana or a sprinkle of ground cinnamon, if desired.
6. Serve immediately and enjoy!

Notes :

1.5 cups frozen banana chunks: 210 calories, 0.8g fat, 54g carbs, 2.6g protein, 6.5g fiber
2 oz premium rum: 128 calories, 0g fat, 0g carbs, 0g protein
Dash of ground cinnamon: negligible calories, fat, carbs, or protein
1/2 cup ice: negligible calories, fat, carbs, or protein
Total calorie count: 338 calories

LIME MARGARITA

There is nothing more fun when choosing to day drink with friends than to put margaritas on the mix. It could be very refreshing to have a cocktail, and have a dip in the ocean. I am known to have a drink and then go swim some laps. Life feels fun when you can sip this citrusy beverage and hang out with your friends.

Ingredients :

2 oz premium tequila. (For a

different Vibe, swap gin for

tequila but do not mix both)

1 oz fresh lime juice

1 oz triple sec

1/2 oz sugar-free simple syrup

(e.g. Lakanto or similar brand)

Ice

Notes :

2 oz premium tequila: 128 calories, 0g fat, 0g carbs, 0g protein
1 oz fresh lime juice: 8 calories, 0g fat, 2.6g carbs, 0.2g protein, 0.2g fiber
1 oz triple sec: 73 calories, 0g fat, 6.5g carbs, 0g protein
1 tsp sugar alternative: negligible calories, fat, carbs, or protein
Salt rim and ice: negligible calories, fat, carbs, or protein
Total calorie count: 209 calories

Procedure :

1. Add the tequila, fresh lime juice, triple sec, and sugar alternative to a cocktail shaker.

2. Fill the shaker with ice.

3. Shake vigorously for 10-15 seconds until the outside of the shaker is frosty.

4. Strain the margarita into a salt-rimmed glass filled with ice.

5. Garnish with a wedge of lime.

6. Serve and enjoy!.

BLOODY CESEAR

This is a popular cocktail of choice around the world and certainly in the Lewis Family. We have enjoyed this for generations. It is interesting to note that there are quick servings of this but also that there are ways to keep it more fresh using natural ingredients and flavorings. You can mix up the alcohol of choice or for a fun swap; try tequila instead of vodka. The main note is not to mix spirits but choose one and keep it clean.

Ingredients :

1.5 oz organic vodka
4 oz organic tomato juice
1 tsp organic Worcestershire sauce
1 tsp organic horseradish
1 tsp organic hot sauce
1/2 tsp organic celery salt
1/4 tsp organic black pepper
Juice of 1/2 organic lime
Organic pickled veggies, such as pickled asparagus, green beans, or okra
Organic celery stalk, for garnish
Ice

Notes :

1.5 oz organic vodka: 97 calories, 0g fat, 0g carbs, 0g protein
4 oz organic tomato juice: 40 calories, 0g fat, 10g carbs, 2g protein, 2g fiber
1 tsp organic Worcestershire sauce: negligible calories, fat, carbs, or protein
1 tsp organic horseradish: negligible calories, fat, carbs, or protein
1 tsp organic hot sauce: negligible calories, fat, carbs, or protein
1/2 tsp organic celery salt: negligible calories, fat, carbs, or protein
1/4 tsp organic black pepper: negligible calories, fat, carbs, or protein
Juice of 1/2 organic lime: 8 calories, 0g fat, 2.6g carbs, 0.2g protein, 0.2g fiber
Organic pickled veggies and celery stalk: negligible calories, fat, carbs, or protein
Ice: negligible calories, fat, carbs, or protein
Total calorie count: 145 calories

Procedure :

1. Fill a cocktail shaker with ice.

2. Add the organic vodka, organic tomato juice, organic Worcestershire sauce, organic horseradish, organic hot sauce, organic celery salt, organic black pepper, and the juice of 1/2 organic lime to the shaker.

3. Shake vigorously for 10-15 seconds until the outside of the shaker is frosty.

4. Strain the mixture into an organic, salt-rimmed glass filled with ice.

5. Garnish with organic pickled veggies and an organic celery stalk.

6. Serve and enjoy!

TEQUILA SOUR

This cocktail is fabulous and refreshing to enjoy at the pool side or for a day at the beach. You can make a jug of the juice mix and have a supplementary addition of your spirits and ice of choice.

Ingredients :

2 oz premium tequila (alternatively you can choose vodka)

2 oz fresh grapefruit juice

Juice of 1/2 lemon

1 sprig of fresh rosemary or thyme

Dash sparkling water

Ice

Grapefruit or lemon slice, for garnish

Procedure :

1. Fill a cocktail shaker with ice.
2. Add 2 oz vodka, 2 oz fresh grapefruit juice, and the juice of 1/2 lemon to the shaker.
3. Strip the leaves off the bottom of the fresh herb sprig and add to the shaker.
4. Shake vigorously for 10-15 seconds until the outside of the shaker is frosty.
5. Strain the mixture into a glass filled with ice.
6. Top off the glass with sparkling water.
7. Garnish with a grapefruit or lemon slice and the remaining fresh herb sprig.
8. Serve and enjoy!

Notes :

2 oz vodka: 97 calories, 0g fat, 0g carbs, 0g protein
2 oz fresh grapefruit juice: 25 calories, 0g fat, 6g carbs, 0.5g protein, 0.5g fiber
Juice of 1/2 lemon: 8 calories, 0g fat, 2.6g carbs, 0.2g protein, 0.2g fiber
1 sprig of fresh rosemary or thyme: negligible calories, fat, carbs, or protein
Sparkling water: negligible calories, fat, carbs, or protein
Ice: negligible calories, fat, carbs, or protein
Grapefruit or lemon slice: negligible calories, fat, carbs, or protein
Total calorie count: 130 calories

Sweet Tooth
Solutions

OATMEAL COOKIE

COOKIES

These cookies were inspired when I was spending some time with my brother and his family and the kids loved baking during the lockdown. Nothing like a healthy cookie to have around the house with kids.

SERVINGS	TIME	DIFFICULTY	CALORIES
24	30 min	Easy	155 kcal

INGREDIENTS

1 cup gluten-free oats

2 tbsp. ground flax seeds

1 cup sugar or sugar alternative

1 cup vegan butter or vegetable oil

½ tsp fine sea salt

1 tbsp. ginger powder or tea powder

½ cup nut butter (optional)

1 tsp pure vanilla extract

¼ cup chocolate chips (optional, dairy-free and sugar-free)

1 tsp cinnamon for sprinkle (optional)

NOTES

DIRECTIONS

1. Preheat the oven to 350°F and line a baking sheet with parchment paper.
2. In a mixing bowl, combine the gluten-free oats and ground flax seeds.
3. In a separate mixing bowl, cream together the sugar and vegan butter or coconut oil until smooth.
4. Add the fine sea salt, ginger powder or tea powder, nut butter (if using), and pure vanilla extract to the sugar mixture, and stir to combine.
5. Add the oat mixture to the sugar mixture and stir until well combined.
6. If using, fold in the dairy-free and sugar-free chocolate chips.
7. Use a cookie scoop or spoon to drop the dough onto the lined baking sheet.
8. Sprinkle with cinnamon (if using).
9. Bake for 10-12 minutes or until the edges are lightly golden brown.
10. Allow the cookies to cool for a few minutes on the baking sheet before transferring them to a wire rack to cool completely.
11. Your gluten-free ginger oat cookies are now ready to be enjoyed as a sweet and healthy treat!

Nutrition Facts: Serving Size: 1 cookie (assuming 24 cookies) Calories: 155 kcal Total Fat: 10g. Saturated Fat: 5g
Trans Fat: 0g Cholesterol: 0mg Sodium: 78mg Total Carbohydrates: 16g Dietary Fiber: 1g Sugars: 9g
Protein: 2g Vitamin D: 0mcg Calcium: 8mg Iron: 0.5mg Potassium: 54mg
Please note that these are only estimated nutrition and calorie facts and may vary depending on the exact ingredients and quantities used. Also, these values do not include the optional ingredients like nut butter, chocolate chips, and cinnamon. It's always recommended to consult a registered dietitian or healthcare professional for accurate and personalized nutrition advice.

CHOCOLATE CHIP COOKIES AND COCONUT ICE CREAM

CHOC CHIP

GLUTEN FREE

Cookies are fun to bake and yes, they can add up with calories quickly, so nothing like keeping mindful consumption and indulging once in a while with the people you love.

SERVINGS	TIME	DIFFICULTY	CALORIES
18	30 min	Easy	180 kcal per cookie

INGREDIENTS

1 stick butter or vegan butter, at room temperature

¼ cup maple syrup or agave

½ cup light brown sugar

1 tsp vanilla essence

1 large egg or 1 tbsp. ground flax and 3 tbsp. water/ ½ cup mashed banana

1 heaping cup of gluten-free all-purpose flour

1 cup semi-sweet dairy-free chocolate chips

Optional: 1/4 cup vegan coconut ice cream for serving.

NOTES

DIRECTIONS

1. Preheat the oven to 350°F and line a baking sheet with parchment paper.
2. In a large mixing bowl, cream together the butter, maple syrup or agave, and light brown sugar until light and fluffy.
3. Add the vanilla essence and egg (or flax mixture or mashed banana) and mix until well combined.
4. Add the gluten-free all-purpose flour and mix until just combined.
5. Fold in the dairy-free chocolate chips.
6. Use a cookie scoop or spoon to drop the dough onto the lined baking sheet.
7. Bake for 12-15 minutes or until lightly golden brown around the edges.
8. Allow the cookies to cool for a few minutes on the baking sheet before transferring them to a wire rack to cool completely.
9. Serve with ice-cream for your favorite treat when friends come over or with your family for movie night.

Calories: ~180 kcal Total Fat: 9g
Saturated Fat: 5g Trans Fat: 0g Cholesterol: 0mg (if using vegan egg substitute) Sodium: 85mg Total
Carbohydrates: 26g Dietary Fiber: 1g Sugars: 15g Protein: 1g Vitamin D: 0%* Calcium: 1%* Iron: 4%*
*Percent Daily Values (DV) are based on a 2,000-calorie diet.

HEALTHY BANANA BREAD

BANANA BREAD GLUTEN FREE

The lockdown craze, how can anyone forget about baking banana bread during covid. This was the recipe I created and I hope you like it.

SERVINGS	TIME	DIFFICULTY	CALORIES
2	30 min	Easy	215 kcal

INGREDIENTS

1/4 cup vegetable oil

1/4 cup monk fruit sweetener/brown sugar/honey or sweetener of choice

3 ripe bananas

1/2 tsp vanilla extract

1/2 cup almond meal/flour

1/2 cup cassava flour

1/4 cup coconut flour

1/2 tsp baking powder

1/4 tsp sallt

1 Tbsp. Lakanto maple syrup

1/2 tsp cinnamon

1/8 tsp nutmeg

1/2 cup chopped walnuts

1/2 banana thinly sliced for topping

4 tbsp. chopped walnuts

1 tbsp. Lakanto maple syrup

NOTES

DIRECTIONS

1. Preheat oven to 350°F (175°C).
2. In a large bowl, mash the ripe bananas with a fork until smooth.
3. Add the vegetable oil, sweetener, and vanilla extract to the bowl and mix until combined.
4. In a separate bowl, whisk together the almond meal/flour, cassava flour, coconut flour, baking powder, salt, cinnamon, and nutmeg.
5. Add the dry ingredients to the wet ingredients and stir until just combined.
6. Fold in the chopped walnuts.
7. Grease a loaf pan with cooking spray and pour in the batter.
8. Arrange the thinly sliced banana on top of the batter.
9. In a small bowl, mix together the chopped walnuts and Lakanto maple syrup. Sprinkle the mixture over the top of the banana slices.
10. Bake for 50-60 minutes or until a toothpick inserted into the center of the bread comes out clean.
11. Let the bread cool for 10-15 minutes before slicing and serving.

Nutrition facts per serving (serves 10):

Calories: 215 Total Fat: 13g Saturated Fat: 2g Cholesterol: 0mg Sodium: 94mg Total Carbohydrates: 19g Dietary Fiber: 3g

Sugars: 5g Protein: 4g

Note: Nutrition facts may vary depending on the type and amount of sweetener used.

CUPCAKES

MINI CUPCAKES   GLUTENFREE

Baking as a kid was so much fun for me. Vanilla cupcakes were my go-to when practicing with my kiddie cookbook. The mini cupcake pan made it all so much more fun. This was a favorite to take to school to share with friends.

SERVING	TIME	DIFFICULTY	CALORIES
28	30 MIN	EASY	287 kcal

INGREDIENTS

1 cup Bob's Red Mill cassava flour

1/2 tsp baking soda

1/2 tsp salt

1/2 cup vegan butter, softened

1/2 cup coconut sugar

1/4 cup honey

2 tsp molasses

1 large egg

1 large egg yolk

2 tsp vanilla extract

1/2 cup unsweetened almond milk

DIRECTIONS

1. Preheat oven to 350°F and line a cupcake tin or mini cupcake tin with liners.
2. In a medium mixing bowl, whisk together cassava flour, baking soda, and salt.
3. In a large mixing bowl, cream together vegan butter, coconut sugar, honey, and molasses until light and fluffy.
4. Add egg, egg yolk, and vanilla extract to the butter mixture and beat until well combined.
5. Gradually add dry ingredients to the wet mixture, alternating with almond milk, and beat until well combined.
6. Pour the batter into cupcake liners, filling each about 2/3 full.
7. Bake for 18-20 minutes or until a toothpick inserted into the center comes out clean.
8. Allow the cupcakes to cool completely before frosting.

NOTES

Based on the ingredients listed in the edited recipe, here is an estimated nutrition information for one vanilla cupcake: Calories: 287 Total Fat: 17g Saturated Fat: 8g Cholesterol: 45mg Sodium: 313mg Total Carbohydrates: 32g Dietary Fiber: 1g Sugars: 23g Protein: 2g

CANNABIS BROWNIES

SPACE CAKES VEGAN

When it comes to having brownies, it is always a good idea to get some fun involved while keeping it healthy and gluten free. Now you can make these plain or include some medicinals.

SERVINGS	TIME	DIFFICULTY	CALORIES
2	30 MIN	EASY	169 kcal

INGREDIENTS

½ cup cannabis-infused coconut oil

1/8 cup coconut oil, vegan butter, or butter

¼ cup peanut butter or sunflower seed butter

¼ cup plus 2 tbsp. raw sugar or sweetener of choice

1/3 cup syrup of choice (agave or yacon)

¾ cup unsweetened cocoa powder

1 tsp pure vanilla extract

¼ tsp Himalayan sea salt

2 eggs

½ cup finely ground almond flour

½ cup vegan sugar-free chocolate chips (optional)

DIRECTIONS

1. Preheat the oven to 350°F and line an 8x8 inch baking pan with parchment paper.
2. In a microwave-safe bowl, combine the cannabis-infused coconut oil, coconut oil/vegan butter or butter, and peanut butter or sunflower seed butter. Heat in the microwave for 30 seconds or until melted.
3. Stir in the sweetener and syrup until well combined.
4. Add the cocoa powder, vanilla extract, and Himalayan sea salt, and mix until fully combined.
5. Add the eggs one at a time, mixing well after each addition.
6. Stir in the finely ground almond flour and mix until just combined.
7. If desired, stir in the vegan sugar-free chocolate chips.
8. Pour the batter into the lined baking pan and smooth out the top.
9. Bake for 25-30 minutes, or until the edges are set and the center is still slightly gooey.
10. Allow the brownies to cool completely in the pan before slicing and serving.

NOTES

Calories: 169 kcal Total Fat: 14g Saturated Fat: 8g Trans Fat: 0g Cholesterol: 27mg Sodium: 69mg Total Carbohydrates: 10g Dietary Fiber: 3g Sugars: 5g Protein: 4g Vitamin D: 0mcg Calcium: 27mg Iron: 1mg Potassium: 136mg

CASSAVA PONE BAJAN

This gluten free treat comes from old school history Barbados and is yummy, filling, and a family favorite.
It is quite calorie dense so you can expect that it could even be a great quick breakfast choice to replace a
low fiber muffin, these are packed with fiber.

SERVINGS	TIME	DIFFICULTY	CALORIES
2	30 min	Easy	315 kcal

INGREDIENTS

4 cups grated cassava

1/2 cup grated coconut

1/2 cup coconut sugar

1/2 cup melted coconut oil

1/2 cup almond milk

1 tsp ground cinnamon

1 tsp grated nutmeg

1 tsp vanilla extract

1/2 tsp salt

2 tbsp. dark rum

2 tbsp. coconut flour

1 tbsp. baking powder

1/2 cup raisins

NOTES

DIRECTIONS

1. Preheat oven to 350°F (180°C).

2. In a large bowl, combine the grated cassava, grated coconut, coconut sugar, melted coconut oil, almond milk, cinnamon, nutmeg, vanilla extract, salt, and rum.

3. In a separate bowl, whisk together the coconut flour and baking powder, then add to the cassava mixture and mix well.

4. Stir in the raisins.

5. Pour the mixture into a greased 9x13 inch baking dish and smooth the top with a spatula.

6. Bake for 50-60 minutes, or until the pone is golden brown and a toothpick inserted into the center comes out clean.

7. Let the pone cool for at least 30 minutes before slicing and serving.

8. Enjoy your delicious Barbados Cassava Pone!

During Covid, I did some recipe testing with a health coach and this was by far one of our favorites. I feel the world could do with a little tropical bliss. Calories per serving: 315 Total Fat: 20 g Saturated Fat: 15 g Cholesterol: 0 mg Sodium: 218 mg Total Carbohydrates: 34 g Dietary Fiber: 2 g Total Sugars: 15 g Protein: 1 g

CANNABIS RICE CRISPIES

RICE CRISPIES   CHEWY GOOEY

So edibles are always fun when hanging out with friends on the weekend. Nothing like getting spaced out but you can also edit this recipe for the normal rice crispy version.

SERVINGS	TIME	DIFFICULTY	CALORIES
16	30 min	Easy	180 kcal

INGREDIENTS

4 cups rice crispies

3 packs marshmallows

1/2 cup cannabis butter

1/4 cup coconut oil

DIRECTIONS

1. In a large saucepan, melt the cannabis butter and coconut oil over low heat.
2. Add the marshmallows and stir until they are completely melted and combined with the butter and oil.
3. Remove the pan from the heat and stir in the rice crispies, making sure they are evenly coated with the marshmallow mixture.
4. Transfer the mixture to a 9x13 inch baking dish lined with parchment paper or lightly greased with cooking spray.
5. Use a spatula or your hands to press the mixture evenly into the dish.
6. Allow the rice crispy treats to cool and set for at least 30 minutes before slicing and serving.

NOTES

Serving size: 1 square (assuming 16 servings). Calories: 180
Total Fat: 7g Saturated Fat: 5g Cholesterol: 15mg Sodium: 150mg Total Carbohydrates: 28g Dietary Fiber: 0g
Sugars: 16g Protein: 1g

GRANOLA BARS

GRANOLA   AMAZING SNACK

Granola bars are amazing to make for the week whether you live with room mates or a family. Even if you are an independent person, these are great for meal prep for a busy work week.

SERVINGS	TIME	DIFFICULTY	CALORIES
15	35 min	Easy	272 kcal

INGREDIENTS

1/3 cup ground raw almonds

1/3 cup ground raw pecans

1/3 cup ground raw walnuts

1 teaspoon kosher salt

1/2 cup xylitol sweetener or sweetener of choice

1/2 cup dried goji berries or cranberries

2 cups gluten-free old-fashioned rolled oats

2 cups gluten-free puffed rice cereal

4 tablespoons maple syrup

5 tablespoons virgin coconut oil or butter

DIRECTIONS

1. Preheat your oven to 325°F. Line a quarter sheet pan with unbleached parchment paper and set it aside.
2. In a large bowl add all nuts and add to blender to grind.Place the ground almond, ground pecans, ground walnuts, salt and xylitol, and whisk to combine well. Add the oats and puffed rice cereal, and then the syrup and oil, and mix to combine well.
3. Scrape the mixture onto the prepared baking sheet and spread into an even layer. Cover the baking sheet with another sheet of unbleached parchment paper, and place another quarter sheet pan on top of the top sheet of parchment paper. Apply as much even pressure as possible on the top sheet pan to compress the mixture as much as possible.
4. Remove the top quarter sheet pan and the top piece of parchment paper, and place the baking sheet in the center of the preheated oven. Bake for about 25 minutes, or until the bars are evenly golden brown.
5. Remove the baking sheet from the oven and allow the bars cool for 5 minutes before sliding them out on top of the parchment paper and slice into 3 rows of 5 rectangles. Allow to cool completely before separating the bars. They will crisp as they cool, and will hold together well once cool.

NOTES

Calories: 272 Total fat: 15g Saturated fat: 5g Cholesterol: 0mg Sodium: 204mg Total carbohydrate: 31g
Dietary fiber: 5g Total sugars: 9g Protein: 6g

CONCLUSION

In this book, I've offered tropical secrets that you can bring to life in your own environment. When it comes to longevity and being healthy and fulfilled in life, these tips should help with managing day-to-day stresses and finding balance.

During my own journey, friends gave me the nickname Organnick because I was so obsessed with doing this research, improving my own health and wellness, and helping people with their lives. I found a personal balance that works in my lifestyle. But even as a professional, I still have my indulgences and challenges. I encourage you to take this information and think about it, try the recipes, have fun, talk about it with friends, and discover ways to find your green balance.

When it comes to keeping a lean body, it's healthy and important to remember that portions really do matter. Eating three meals a day, including mostly vegetables and a lot of liquids, helps to keep calories down, especially if you're not active. And if you're active, including whole foods will help, especially if you want to build muscle. Remember that there are many tropical ingredients that are available around the world. They will give your diet a variety of textures and tastes so you don't become bored while trying to keep the food you eat simple and balanced. If you practice meal prep once a week, you'll be more likely to eat healthfully. Finding a routine that works for your lifestyle is going to be the ultimate takeaway, because everybody's lifestyle is different.

I'm grateful for everybody who's been on the journey with me. It's come with a lot of hurdles, obstacles, challenges, and sacrifice. Hopefully, it inspires your journey as well. I'm grateful to be around some of the top talent professionals: chefs, vegan and raw-food chefs, trainers, Olympian athletes, functional neurologists, physiotherapists, psychologists, psychotherapists, nutritionists and dieticians, functional practitioners, naturopaths and holistic healers, and professionals in general. Living here, surrounded by these top-tier professionals, has inspired my own journey and the development of these ideas. While this information is written in many different places and disciplines, the uniqueness of these secrets is in the way they are inspired by tropical living. Thank you for being part of it.

Acknowledgements

Expression of Gratitude for Supporters

Clients and People of My Green Balance

Coaches and Mentors, David H and Pitchers

Parents

Barcants, Evendens

Lewis Legends

In Loving Memory of Marilyn & Mervyn Lewis

My Best Friend Nic Puckrin

Wolf Pack

Naimies

Editor Jessica

For further information, write to greenbalancett@gmail.com
www.mygreenbalance.com.

ABOUT THE AUTHOR

Annick Gabrielle Lewis is a wellness and lifestyle coach based in Barbados. She works with clients remotely all over the world.

Annick offers personalized lifestyle planning and accountability,
functional training,
healthy behavior psychology and habit training,
executive wellness, travel and diet, diet plans,
and emotional intelligence and mindfulness training.

Annick helps people move through different types of grief
and lifestyle transitions
(such as retirement, having a baby, or moving to a new house or country)
in order to reconnect with their healthy habits.

For further information, write to greenbalancett@gmail.com
www.mygreenbalance.com.
Work IG ‖ Mygreenbalance
GreenbalancebyOrgannick
Personal Branding IG ‖ Iamorgannick

Printed in the USA
CPSIA information can be obtained
at www.ICGtesting.com
LVHW070353180124
769031LV00007B/192

9 798988 848011